THE ILLUSTRATED ENCYCLOPEDIA OF
BUTTERFLIES
& MOTHS

THE ILLUSTRATED ENCYCLOPEDIA OF
BUTTERFLIES
& MOTHS

By Dr V. J. Staněk

Edited by

Dr Brian Turner

EXCLUSIVE LIBRARY DISTRIBUTORS:

classic
publications

800 VELLA ROAD
PALM SPRINGS
CALIFORNIA 92262

octopus

Text and photographs by Dr V. J. Staněk

Translated by Vera Gissing
Pen drawings by E. Smrčinová

English version first published 1977 by
Octopus Books Limited
59 Grosvenor Street, London W1

ISBN 0 7064 0547 1

Printed in Czechoslovakia
3/11/01/51-01

CONTENTS

WHAT ARE BUTTERFLIES?

The attention of Man has always been focused on butterflies and moths, not only because of their general beauty, striking colours and wondrous shapes, but also because of the amazing variability of form in individual species. These handsome insects are not just the magnificent and conspicuous specimens, often of some considerable size, but also many species less colourful in appearance, such as many moths and a number of the so-called 'minute moths', whose beauty was for a long time neglected being discovered only through more detailed study. These minute butterflies and moths often surpass their bigger brothers in loveliness and colour.

It is not easy to estimate the number of described species of butterflies and moths inhabiting our planet. This is because the exact classification of some species is sometimes hard to determine, and because the number of known butterflies is continually rising with discoveries of new species. The tropics are the most fruitful ground for finding previously unknown species, and the sources are still by no means exhausted; other areas can also provide new discoveries. So the total of 138,000, which is the approximate estimated number of species of butterflies and moths on the Earth, is not final.

This book illustrates the most important and interesting species of Eurasia as well as North America and also exotic species of tropical South America. The selection has been guided by the intention to present to the reader the most interesting facts on basic taxonomy, modes of life and mutual ecological relations of species inhabiting individual geographical areas. Butterflies economically useful or harmful and species endangered by civilization are also mentioned. Attention has been centred on the butterflies' attractiveness of shape and colour, their size, coloration and camouflage, as well as on their most conspicuous caterpillars and pupae. The book has been intended to make the most attractive insects — butterflies and moths — familiar to the reader.

Butterflies and moths belong to the class Insecta (the insects), in the sub-class Pterygota (winged insects) and are included in the super-order Panorpoidea (because of the affinities they show to scorpion fly (Panorpa) larvae. They are grouped in this super-order together with Alder flies (Megaloptera), Snake flies (Raphidiodea), Lacewings (Planipennia), Scorpion flies (Mecoptera), Caddis flies (Trichoptera), true flies (Diptera) and fleas (Siphonaptera), and form the order Lepidoptera — butterflies and moths.

The primitive forms of butterflies and moths resemble Caddis flies in the vein structure of their wings, in the way the wings are joined and in the formation of their mouth parts. They also have a similar covering of body and wings. The Caddis flies are hairy, the butterflies have bodies covered with scales. Some hairs of the Caddis flies actually thicken into scales. One may deduct therefore that Lepidoptera have possibly developed either directly from the Caddis flies, or from an ancestor common to both.

If we are to answer the question posed by the title of this chapter, we must define butterflies and moths as the flying land insects with complete metamorphosis, in which the development of the insect passes through the stages of egg — larva — pupa — and the adult, with four wings covered with coloured scales. The adult (imago) feeds on the nectar from flowers with the aid of its suctorial proboscis. The caterpillars, which are equipped with biting mouth parts, usually feed on growing plants.

The body of a butterfly is divided into three basic sections: the head, the thorax and the abdomen. Like all other insects, the body is supported by an outer casing which is both hard and resilient. Muscles and internal organs are attached to the inner surface of this outer casing, or exoskeleton. Furthermore, the head and the thorax have an internal branch-like framework of struts — the endoskeleton — to which the muscles operating the mouthparts attach. The external casing is composed of a number of chemical substances of which chitin is the most important. Chitin is insoluble in water and does not dissolve even in organic acids. In nature, chitin decomposes in a dead insect body only with the help of specific micro-organisms.

The head is usually limited in movement. Basically it is formed of six segments, the first three being associated with the sensory components of the head with a pair of compound eyes, antennae and simple eyes. The other three head-segments are associated with the mouth parts. In adult insects these segments are usually joined in such a manner that it is hardly possible to tell them apart.

The jaws (mandibles) in most butterflies have been highly reduced so that they have lost their original biting function. Other accessory mouth parts (maxillae) have been adapted for sucking purposes, being transformed into two elongated half tubes, which are held together with hooks so as to form a tubular, hollow sucking and licking organ — the proboscis. When not in use, the proboscis is coiled in a spiral. Towards the end it forms a narrowing capillary, which is split at the tip.

The labial palps have sensitive tips and their function is, undoubtedly, to act as sensory feelers. The shape of the palps and their number of segments are an important identification sign.

The antennae project from the top of the head, and can be moved in all directions. They are usually threadlike, but in some families they are thicker at the tip, or clubbed, or hooked; others are bristle-shaped or comb-like on one or both sides, or are intricately feathered. Delicate nerve cells are located here which function as highly sensitive organs of smell. The antennae are also used as sensory feelers.

The eyes of a butterfly are situated at the sides of the head. They are compound,

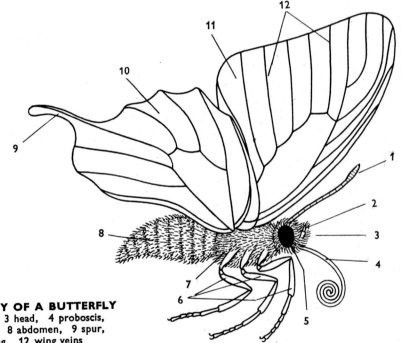

EXTERNAL ANATOMY OF A BUTTERFLY
1 antenna, 2 labial palp, 3 head, 4 proboscis,
5 eye, 6 legs, 7 thorax, 8 abdomen, 9 spur,
10 hind wing, 11 forewing, 12 wing veins

8

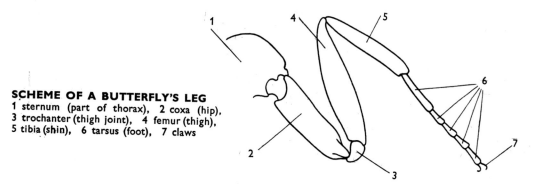

SCHEME OF A BUTTERFLY'S LEG
1 sternum (part of thorax), 2 coxa (hip),
3 trochanter (thigh joint), 4 femur (thigh),
5 tibia (shin), 6 tarsus (foot), 7 claws

faceted, built up from separate optical units, called ommatidia, of which a butterfly can have between twelve and seventeen thousand.

Butterflies seem to have excellent vision, particularly at shorter distances. The swift, powerful fliers are especially noted for being able to move expertly and safely in difficult surroudings full of obstacles. Although other senses aid the butterfly in its flight, vision is undoubtedly the most important one.

Apart from compound eyes, insects frequently have simple eyes — ocelli. Most insects possess three, but butterflies, if these eyes are developed at all, have two, and they are placed at the back of the head, between the antennae and the compound eyes. They are usually hidden by the growth of hairy scales and are seen only when uncovered, and with the aid of a magnifying glass. The function of the simple eyes has not yet been fully determined. It is thought they may enable outline seeing at close quarters, or hold the function similar to exposure metres in photography, or rangefinders in conjunction with compound eyes.

The thorax of butterflies is distinctly separated from the head and the abdomen. It is attached to the head by a delicate short membranous neck, which gives the insect a certain movability and a partial ability to turn the head to the side. The thorax of a butterfly is composed of relatively strong segments which form a hard box, filled largely with muscles. It consists of three basic parts: prothorax, mesothorax and metathorax. The forelegs are attached to the prothorax, whilst the middle legs and the pair of forewings are attached to the mesothorax. The metathorax bears the third pair of legs and the hind wings. The second and third thorax segments which bear the wings are firmly joined in butterflies, thus giving strong support to both pairs of wings. On the sides of the thorax two pairs of respiratory spiracles are situated.

The butterfly leg consists of a short hip (coxa), a still shorter thigh joint (trochanter), a long thigh (femur), a long shin (tibia) and a foot composed of several tarsal segments. The anatomic classification is purely illustrative and does not express in any way a homologous relationship — that is, as far as evolution is concerned, there is no connection with the individual parts of limbs in vertebrates.

The foot usually has five segments and is equipped with two claws. However, the number of segments varies in different species and sexes, or the foot segments are adapted for other purposes. Butterfly feet, particularly the front pair, are often sensitive organs of smell, through which the butterfly takes in the scent of nectar, flowers, or its sexual mate. The individual segments of the legs have various spines or spurs at the joint, which help the butterfly in supporting itself against a solid object or in crawling out of the ground.

The wings (ala, pteron) are the most important organs of locomotion in butterflies. They are the outgrowths of the thorax in the form of two pairs of flat membranous formations reinforced by a network of veins, which are firmly joined with the sides of the second and third thorax segments. At the base of each wing there is a complex system of flat sclerites. These variably shaped strips are most important for the method of flight. Some, together with groups of wing muscles in the thorax, are responsible for the movement of the wings. From the sclerites, reinforcing wing veins branch out radially across the wing. The veins are hollow, firm tubes, filled with blood and trachea in living specimens. Together with nerves, these tracheal tubes interlace practically the whole area of the wing. The wing is composed of the closely attached lower and upper membranes, which form a solid duplicature, and are pulled and held together by connecting strands. The soft limp wings of the newly emerged butterfly are gradually expanded by pumping blood and air into the veins. The wings enlarge to their rightful size and shape, and as soon as they harden, the butterfly is capable of flight. The distribution of wing veins is constant within individual species and is therefore most useful for classification purposes. Butterflies and moths, and many other orders of the sub-class Pterygota, have been classified according to the shape and the presence and distribution of certain specific veins. The vein structure of the scale-covered butterfly wings is generally only slightly discernible or completely indistinguishable, and to see it properly, it is necessary to remove the scales. This necessitates the application of a special technique which, unfortunately, damages or destroys the butterfly. For this reason, this book will not concentrate on giving more detailed characteristics of the wing vein structure. The way the forewings are linked on each side to the hind wings to achieve efficient flight is an important factor in the system of classification and division of the species. Butterflies and moths are able to beat and flutter both wings on either side simultaneously, helped by a special apparatus situated at the basal end of the wings. It is connected with marginal veins and is in fact a membranous protruding lobe projecting from the hind edge of the forewing, which catches under the front edge of the hind wing. This type of coupling is called 'jugate' and is common in the most primitive species. These primitive insects also have a similar vein distribution in the hind and forewing, and are commonly called Homoneura (similarly veined). The other group, Heteroneura (variably veined), which includes most butterflies and moths, have a considerably varied vein pattern on the fore and hind wings. This group differs also in the way the hind wings are attached to the forewings. They have a special device called 'frenulum', which consists of a tuft of tough bristles grouped together to form a flexible spine on the front edge of the hind wing, which is gripped by a catch on the underside of the forewing. Lepidoptera thus equipped are less commonly known under the name of Frenata.

The shape of the wings is roughly triangular, but in many families it varies considerably. The wings of the most powerful fliers, for instance, are narrowed; others are rounded. Sometimes the wing margins are variously cut out, other times the wings form spurs or tassels, or are cleaved into feathery tails. Females may sometimes be wingless.

The wings of Lepidoptera are not hairless. The upper and undersides, the edges and all projections are covered in fine hairs, many of which are transformed into flattened scales. With some of the larger lepidoptera species, it is possible to brush the scales permanently aside and thus expose the glossy surface of the skin.

The shape of the scales varies considerably. They can be almost circular, like fish-scales, long and thin, slate-like, arrow-like with a tooth-edged tail, or fan-like, resembling a palm leaf. Sometimes the scales are also gland-cells, forming short bristles at the distal

10

Various shapes of butterfly scales

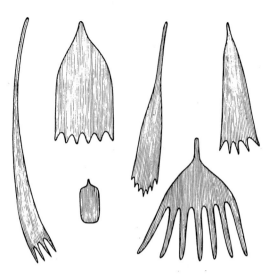

end, or they are arranged as the long-plumed scent scales characteristic of the wings of males.

Butterflies and moths are renowned for the exquisite colour of their wings. The scales give the colour to the wings. In the case of the mat-coloured species, the scales contain a variety of colour pigments which produce the vivid or the dull shades in butterflies and the less conspicuous moths. These 'paints' are complex chemical compounds and sometimes also the vitamins for growth and they dictate the coloration of the species. But the most exquisite butterflies with their brilliant, dazzling coat, owe their beauty to physical factors, particularly to the interference of light in the fine layers of the wings. The scales are by no means compact or simple. When cut across and examined under a microscope, the enormous structural variability of their inner composition comes to light.

Under the dorsal plates of the exoskeleton there is a tubular blood vessel extending from the head along the length of the body. The part of this blood vessel which lies in the abdomen is capable of pumping movements and forms a tubular heart. The anterior part of the blood vessel, which passes through the thorax is called the aorta and conducts blood to the head. The gullet, or oesophagus, extends from the mouth parts, through the thorax running beneath the aorta, and into the abdomen and the rest of the digestive system. The nerve cord, running along the underside of the body is enlarged periodically into subsidiary brains called ganglia. A pair of salivary glands, also situated in the thorax, terminate at the mouth parts.

The abdomen of butterflies and moths is generally firmly and widely attached to the thorax, which is in contrast to some other insect orders where the connection of the two is quite narrow. The lepidopteran abdomen consists usually of ten well defined segments. It is roughly oval in shape, rather soft and has no limbs or appendages. The last segments of the abdomen are, as a rule, firmly joined and modified into sexual organs.

In the soft membranous lateral parts of the segments there are six to seven pairs of respiratory openings called spiracles.

The abdomen contains digestive organs, the heart and associated muscles and membranes, the excretory and sexual organs and a complex muscular system. The central part of the digestive tube is interwoven with the complicated system of tubules of the

Malpighian excretory apparatus. Species which do not feed in the adult state have the greater part of their digestive system filled with air — which serves to reduce the weight of the insect.

The blood leaves the opening of the aorta in the head and passes through the thorax and into the abdomen bathing the internal organs. Blood from the body-cavity is sucked in through the lateral openings (ostioles) of the tubular heart which forces it forwards into the head, and out again into the body-cavity. The tubular heart, which widens in individual abdominal segments, pulsates exceptionally fast in some species. One hundred and fifty beats per minute were recorded in the Privet Hawk-moth (*Sphinx ligustri*) after flight. On the other hand, the fully grown caterpillar of this moth, when at rest, has only forty five heart beats per minute.

The nerve cord runs from the head through the thorax on the underside of the abdomen to the distal end of the body. The number of pairs of ganglia in each body ring corresponds roughly to the number of segments.

In females, the internal sexual organs take up the largest part of the abdomen. Their main components are the pair of ovaries, each consisting of several egg-filled tubes. The finest ends of the tubes are fused together. Here the eggs develop as they pass down these ovarian tubes into the oviducts. Both oviducts merge and from here the eggs pass into a wider part called the vestibulum, where they are fertilized by the male sperms.

After fertilization and still inside the vestibulum the eggs become coated with a sticky secretion, which enables them to stick to a selected surface. The females of some species are not particular as to where they deposit their eggs, but most of them choose appropriate leaves, twigs or flowers with great care.

The male sexual organs consists of two testes which are fused together and which produce the sperms; the sperm ducts carry the sperms towards the copulatory organ, the penis.

The last two or three abdominal segments no longer look like normal body-rings, for they have been adapted to form external copulation organs. These are highly complicated structures in both females and males which help the two sexual partners to clasp one another by their tail ends. Their fusion can be so strong, that the pair remain locked together for many hours. Moths often remain joined after the night has ended, right through the longer part of the next day, sometimes up to the evening.

THE LIFE CYCLE OF BUTTERFLIES AND MOTHS

There are four stages in the life cycle of a butterfly: egg, caterpillar, pupa and adult.

EGG

After fertilization, the female butterflies or moths generally select suitable places in nature for depositing their eggs (ova). In captivity they usually deposit them on walls of the container where they are kept. But some species refuse to lay eggs in captivity and choose to die instead. The eggs of each species are of a specific size, shape and number. The size of a batch in butterflies and moths is quoted as containing between 25 to 10,000 eggs. The size of the egg fluctuates between 0.5 mm in diameter to a little over 3 mm, and is relatively constant in each species. The shape of the eggs is varied

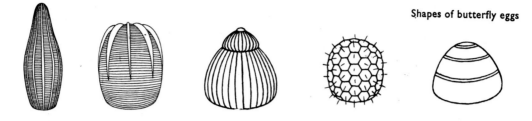

and they can be globular, disc-like, conical, barrel-shaped, melon-shaped, bottle-shaped, angular or typically egg-shaped. The females of some species lay their eggs singly, others cover the chosen area with neat rows, or lay just a single row. Some form chains or ringlets around twigs, slip them behind bark of trees or into cracks, or lay them in groups. Sometimes the eggs are left exposed, glued to the selected base, while females of other species cover theirs with a blanket of hairs which they free from their abdominal surface. Such a covering makes them inconspicuous, almost invisible. The eggs, as a rule, are not completely smooth. Their surface is often decorated with intricate, ornamental patterns, rather like a Gothic ribbed vault. Fine ribbing generally stretches over the surface of the egg, starting from its end or its centre; the ribs are interlaced with cross-stripes, and the number of both is characteristic for individual species. At the top of the egg there is a shallow depression, the micro-pyle. The microscopic structure of this area is much finer than the lateral ribbing and its design is again typical of the various types.

Caterpillars of the Buff-tip Moth (*Phalera bucephala*) on the underside of an oak leaf

In the middle of this depression there is a minute hole leading into the egg's interior, through which the sperm enters during fertilization.

The shells of all Lepidoptera eggs are chitinous; some are relatively soft, but more often they are fairly hard, resilient and firm, able to withstand changes of weather and surroundings, particularly during hibernation. The coloration of the eggs is also diverse — they come in all possible colours. They often match the colour of the particular place where they have been deposited. While they are ripening, the coloration frequently changes. In most butterflies it is not uniform, but broken by regular or irregular spots. The females of one particular species can lay eggs variably coloured, so the colour of the eggs is not a reliable guide in distinguishing to which species they belong.

The chitinous shell of the egg is commonly transparent, so the changes in coloration of the contents are clearly visible. The transparency and the gloss of the actual shell is best seen after the caterpillar has hatched, but many caterpillars eat their shells then. The time it takes for a caterpillar to hatch can also be very varied and depends greatly on temperature, dampness and the actual species. Caterpillars of some tropical species hatch on the third day after the eggs had been laid, whereas in some of the cooler zones the eggs of many species hibernate, and it takes several months before the caterpillars hatch.

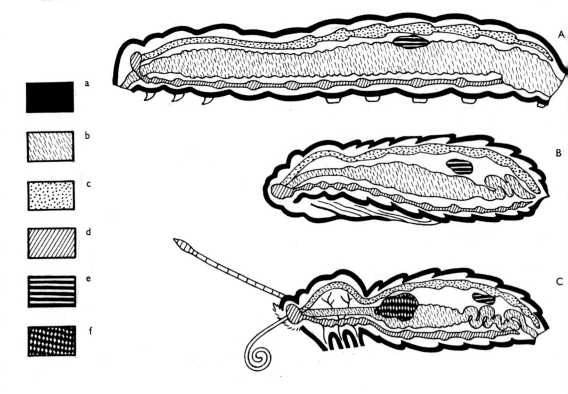

INTERNAL ANATOMY OF A BUTTERFLY
a/ chitinous surface layer, b/ digestive system, c/ blood circulation, d/ nervous system, e/ internal male sexual organs, f/ crop

Arrangement of important internal organs in A/ caterpillar, B/ pupa, C/ adult

CATERPILLAR

The second stage in the development of Lepidoptera is the larva, or caterpillar. Its body is elongate and generally with a soft, flexible skin. The body surface is usually covered in hair, sometimes sparsely, other times thickly. Even the seemingly 'bald' caterpillars have some hair, though it is hardly visible and often very thinly scattered over the body, so this is hardly worth mentioning when describing such caterpillars. On the other hand, when the identification of some butterflies is in dispute, these very hairs can be the most vital characteristics in their classification. The system in which certain bristles or hairs are distributed on the caterpillar's body is called chaetotaxy.

The general arrangement of the caterpillar's internal organs is similar to that of the adult butterfly. The aorta with the tubular heart runs the length of the body along the back, just below the skin. The wide digestive pipe passes from the strongly hardened head through the whole of the body. In the hind part of the body it is surrounded by fine intestine organs known as the Malpighian tubules. The nervous system is situated ventrally under the digestive pipe. In the hind part of the caterpillar's body, between the digestive pipe and the tubular heart, are the rudiments of the reproductive organs — the gonads. The head, which is clearly distinguishable from the rest of the body, bears powerful, complicated toothed jaws (mandibles) which are designed for biting food — flowers, leaves, pulp and wood. On each side of the mouthparts are six larval simple eyes — ocelli, which structurally resemble the individual ommatidia, the optical units of which the facetted eye of the adult butterfly is composed. The caterpillar's body consists of as many as thirteen or fourteen segments. Three segments next to the head form the thorax and each segment bears a pair of strongly hardened jointed legs ending in a claw. The remaining segments are those of the abdomen. Some of them are provided with a pair of false legs, or pro-legs. The last pair are called 'claspers'. The pro-legs end in a contractile pad surrounded by a ring of hooks, which are connected with muscles.

Caterpillars of some of the Lepidoptera (the Tiger-moths, for instance), are capable of running very fast and very persistently.

On the sides of the caterpillar's body are breathing holes called spiracles. In the fore-part of the caterpillar's body the large salivary glands are located. The orifice of the salivary duct lies between the mandibles at the base of the head. The salivary glands produce a liquid which, when in contact with air, instantly solidifies into a strong, resilient thread called silk. The silk thread is essential to caterpillars. Before each moulting they spin a pad of silk to which they attach themselves. Some use the silk to draw together the leaves in which they hide; others descend from trees with the aid of the silk thread, or pupate in the silk cocoon, or use the thread to attach the loose pupa to a firm object.

The larvae, during their development, may shed their skin four to five times or even more and their appearance and coloration often changes with the moulting. The new, looser body covering allows for growth, so that eventually the caterpillar reaches its final size. At the end of the larval stage the caterpillar stops feeding, empties its gut, attaches itself to a pad, or crawls into the ground. Other species spin a cocoon and after a certain period of rest, they shed their skin and change into a pupa.

PUPA — CHRYSALIS

The sheath in which the definite form of the future butterfly is formed is called chrysalis, or pupa. It is generally a fairly firm, hard, oval-shaped formation which is usually narrowed into a tip in the hind part. In the pupal stage the butterfly does not feed, does not moult and does not usually move. Only a few species react when being touched by a slight movement of the abdominal segments. The pupa breathes through the lateral spiracles. There is a pair situated in the thorax, and a pair in each of the clearly separated abdominal segments. The transformation into the adult butterfly within the chrysalis occurs gradually, with the dissolution of some of the larval organic tissues (histolysis) and gradual alteration and the growth of new, definite organs from tiny groups of cells known as imaginal buds. To achieve this, the pupae need specific temperatures at a specific time and many species from cooler regions need temperatures below freezing point for their successful development. The vital internal organs remain roughly in the same position as in the caterpillar through the pupal stage and in the adult butterfly. It is mostly the details, and the final design of the imago which are altered and set inside the pupa. When observing the pupa from the outside, it is possible to see most of the important parts of the future butterfly on the surface. The sclerotized covering of the eyes and legs on the front part of the pupa are clearly mapped out. The future proboscis may be seen running between the stretched-out legs along the underside of the pupa towards the hind end. The wings are also already marked out, and definite, and mini-mized wing venation is often visible. The head of the pupa forms an immobile whole with the thorax. The abdominal segments are slightly movable, but only to the side. There are several different types of pupae in Lepidoptera. The pupae of the most primitive species have the highest movability. Sometimes even the leg cases are slightly free, but the main movement occurs in the coarse abdominal rings which help the pupae to push themselves out of wood-holes in the case of Root-borers, Goat moths and Clearwings. In the case of some other moths these movable rings help them to bore their way out of the firm material on which they used to feed as caterpillars — such as felt, leather, dried fruit. Similar equipment aids the Burnet-moth to push the pupa out of the cocoon during emergence.

The shapes and coloration of pupae are as varied as the butterflies themselves. The pupae of butterflies are particularly known for the characteristic hollows and grooves, ledges, hooks and horns, or glossy golden patches and the most exquisite colours. The shape and coloration of many pupae are perfected examples of camouflage. They merge with their surrounding which protects them against insect-eating predators.

Some caterpillars pupate in various shelters, under moss or in the ground. Many of the moths spin a cocoon before pupating, which at times is so firm that it looks like a narrow strip on the bark of a tree (the Prominents, for instance), or like a lump of sandstone (the Shark moths).

With experience, it is possible to tell beforehand the sex of the future imago by ex-amining the tail end of the underside of the pupa. In the male the margin between the anal opening and the genital opening is shorter than in the female, whose genital opening is situated on a more distant abdominal segment.

The tail end of the pupa is commonly pointed and elongated, but often varies in detail. Sometimes it ends with a smooth disc, sometimes with a sharp point. In species which pupate in the hanging position, this tail end, called the cremaster, is equipped with a system of strong and resilient hooks. These help to secure the pupa to the base by the silk threads spun by the caterpillar before pupating. This equipment also helps during the process of emergence by keeping the pupa shell inside the cocoon and easing the extrication of the butterfly.

The emerging butterfly makes a hole in the thin cover above its head and inhales air

16

through the mouth, filling its digestive system. At the same time, as the skin of the pupa splits, it crawls out carefully, withdrawing its legs, antennae and proboscis. When the legs are free, the butterfly stands up and extracts its wings out of the shell. Then it is generally very easy to extricate the rest of the body. In some species during the emergence, in others not until the wings have fully expanded and hardened, the butterfly or moth ejects from the anus the stored-up excretory products of the Malpighian tubules. These products take the form of a thin, opaque liquid called the meconium, which does not smell and is coloured pink or orange. Not till then is the butterfly ready to take its first flight.

WHAT DO BUTTERFLIES AND MOTHS LIVE ON?

Most adult butterflies and moths feed on nectar from flowers. They either sit directly on the blooms, or cling to the whole inflorescence, probing the individual cups with their proboscis. Sometimes they suck the nectar from within the deeper parts of flowers, pushing their probosces deep down into the interior where the nectar accumulates. The species which feed from flowers with long corolla tubes or long spurs have their tongues appropriately developed, and often elongated to an unusual degree. This is particularly noticeable in Hawk-moths. They do not rest on the blossoms, but suck the nectar whilst in flight, hovering above them like hummingbirds. Moths, as a rule, rest on the blooms and search for nectar with swift movements of their probosces. The mouth parts of many of the moths are so underdeveloped that they are unable to feed or drink during their short lifespan. Quite a few species enjoy feeding on over-ripe, fallen fruit.

However, nectar and the sweet juices are not the only diet of the Lepidoptera. Some species are more inclined to suck the sap from wounded trees, sharing the feast with beetles such as the Rose beetles and Stag beetles, and with flies and hornets. Some of the most exquisite species, particularly the Fritillaries, surprisingly show a preference to foul smelling matter, such as dung, carrion and rotting plant material. Some of the most beautiful examples of *Ornithoptera* can be caught on rubbish heaps. Many exquisite butterflies can be trapped on fresh droppings of large mammals.

Butterflies and moths also need water. They are fond of sucking it from damp, sandy or muddy places. The wandering species, such as the migrating Hawk-moths, particularly enjoy such a refreshing drink after their long, exhausting flight.

A healthy butterfly with a fully developed proboscis cannot exist without food to keep in good physical condition. When in captivity, butterflies and moths very rarely feed themselves. It is, however, possible to strengthen a weakened butterfly with nourishment. Place a few drops of diluted honey on a coarse ledge of a small dish; hold the butterfly by its closed wings and uncurl the proboscis with a needle, then dip the tip into the liquid. Immediately the butterfly will start to suck hungrily. In a little while, without having to extract the tongue out of the honey, the butterfly will sit willingly by the drops and will feed independently. It can be induced to take clean water in the same manner.

Butterfly collectors are known to paste 'bait' on barks of trees and stones in natural suitable localities and hunt there day and night. With the greatest of care they prepare various 'magical' mixtures, boiling them and improving them according to their experiences, by the addition of different tempting ingredients to lure and trap the rarest of species. They often jealously guard the secret of these concoctions. Generally they boil together dark ale, honey, syrup and unpeeled apples, processing it into a thick pulp. The success of such a hunt, especially during the night, depends largely on weather conditions; the best time to catch butterflies and moths is before a storm.

During this century a most unusual and interesting fact has been discovered and proved; certain species, particularly of some moth families, the Loopers, the Prominents, or from the family Pyralidae, live on juices from the eyes of large terrestrial mammals, and therefore also of man. For this reason some members of the order Lepidoptera have to be classified as parasitic. Some species only lick the tears which trickle from the eyes and suck the eye secretion. The probosces of others are equipped with tiny, saw-like teeth to irritate and pierce the mucous membrane, which induces blood capillaries to tear and causes bleeding.

We can see that most Lepidoptera feed on liquid food using their probosces. But there is one primitive family — the Micropterygidae - which lives on solid food, pollen from flowers. These minute, inconspicuous butterflies, are very like moths and are closely related to the Caddis flies. Their mouth parts are well adapted for crushing the pollen grains, and consist of mandibles with teeth and a small basket to hold the pollen.

The caterpillars of butterflies and moths have a much wider menu. Most species depend on a particular plant species and feed mostly on its leaves. Others are not very particular in their choice and go from one to another, often completely unrelated plant. Some caterpillars live on the roots, some on stalks and others on the pulpy parts of plants. There are species which devour only the upper layers of leaves and others which prefer buds and fruit. The caterpillars of Goat moths, Root-borers and Clearwings feed on wood. They bore tunnels similarly to wood-eating beetles (the long horned beetles, or the buprestid beetles, etc.). There are many known species of the Tortrix moths which cause 'worminess' in fruit. From the enormous family Pyralidae we can recall species which attack pantries and stores and which are minute, but dreaded pests. These destructive caterpillars attack anything from dried mushrooms, dried fruit, flour, stale pastries, woollen goods to valuable furs with their delicate but expert mouth parts. One species of this family is associated with live sloths. It was originally thought that the eggs were laid on the sloth fur so the mammal was 'moth-eaten' while it was still alive. This has recently been shown not to be true. The moths use the sloths to carry them to where the sloth defecates. The moths then leave the sloth and lay their eggs in the sloth dung where the larvae develop. Some 'moths' bore holes in the horns of ruminants, just like true parasites. The caterpillars of some of the Pyralidae feed on bee, or on bumble-bee honeycomb, others eat their way through birds' nests.

Hardly ever is it mentioned that caterpillars also drink. One must not forget this when rearing them at home. The caterpillars which live on low-growing plants among grass, have the opportunity to drink from the dew drops. The necessity of water is quite evident in the Drinker of the Eggar family, whose caterpillars must drink in order to develop properly.

Because caterpillars, on the whole, live only for a very short time and feed very intensively, some species can be very serious and destructive pests. Luckily these are in minority and the majority of butterflies and moths are harmless, in fact often useful. The silk industry is actually built on cultivating certain species. Apart from pollinating plants, butterflies and moths have their place of importance in the complex ecological chain of nature. Last, but not least, they are one of its most unique decorations.

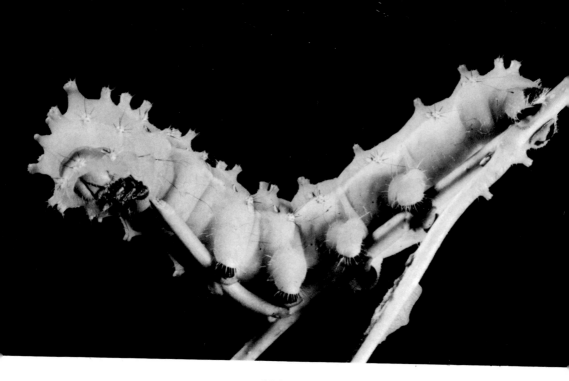

Adult caterpillar of the Greater Emperor Moth (*Saturnia pyri*)

HOW NATURE PROTECTS BUTTERFLIES AND MOTHS

The flight of butterflies and moths, which is often extremely swift, protects them from pursuers. Anyone who has tried to catch butterflies with a net knows that a collector must often be an effective sportsman in order to succeed. If a butterfly realizes it is being pursued, it generally saves itself by flying into the distance, or soaring high, where it is safe from danger. But, because many eventually return to the very same spot, a well-thought out manoeuvre by the collector often brings success. Butterflies and moths can be in good flying condition and alert only when they are physically fresh, when they are in optimum temperature and when it is the time of day or night which is most favourable for their activities. There are many attractive tropical species which are extremely difficult to catch, so collectors often think up various tricks to trap them. On the other hand species such as the mountain-dwelling Apollos, are very easy to catch. They either feebly flutter round blossoms, or they are found resting upon them. Many butterflies and moths are not protected against man, who originally was not their enemy. They are, however, often excellently protected against birds and other insect-eating vertebrates by being permeated with sharp, distasteful chemicals. In fact many species of distant families, which are completely unrelated to the Heliconidae and Danaidae families which have these characteristics, resemble the latter in size, colour and design, although their bodies do not contain the foul-tasting liquid. The outer resemblance to an obnoxious species is often sufficient to put off a predator. Such an occurrence is called mimicry. The Tiger-moth's coloration is so conspicuous it almost acts as a warning, and furthermore, its body gives off a sharp, foul-smelling liquid.

When attacked, some of the larger species occasionally turn aggressive in their defence. When trapped, the Death's-head Hawk-moth stabs its attacker with its proboscis and at the same time gives out a strange squeaking sound. The reaction of night-flying moths, when hearing the high-frequency 'radar' sounds of hunting bats is also well known: as if stunned, they fall to the ground and often save themselves this way.

A butterfly, or moth, when resting and sitting still, is best protected by showing no movement at all, so it does not attract the predator's attention. In such an instance the protective colouring, known as monochromy, makes the butterfly merge with the bark of trees or the foliage, stones or grass to such a degree that it is almost invisible. In these cases the insect's colours mimic the surroudings. The most exquisitely coloured butterflies generally have their underside in dull colours, so when at rest with their wings closed, they become inconspicuous. This characteristic is common, for instance, in the gayest butterflies of South America and in Fritillaries of central Europe. The design on the underside of the wings imitates various types of tree leaves — green, dead or decaying ones, or the leaves attached by saprophytic fungi, or by parasites which cause irregular pathological marks. This camouflage is so perfect, that phyto-pathologists were able to name the species of the fungi which the butterflies imitated on their wings.

The night-flying moths fold their wings in a roof-like position or spread them open when at rest, and are generally inconspicuously coloured on the upper side. Sometimes even the vivid leaf-green occurs there.

On the other hand, the Tiger-moths are very brightly coloured and their vivid markings tend to disrupt their shape, or to act as a warning. This family and many other moths, such as the Underwings, often have their undersides most strikingly coloured, generally in red, which can have a frightening effect on an enemy if they are attacked. The expressive eyespots on the hind wings of most Emperor moths are the best example of such coloration, and there is no doubt at all that these have a frightening effect. The same applies to the 'owl eyes' on the undersides of the South American 'owlets' of the genus *Caligo*, which fly at dusk. Here their frightening appearance is coupled with the movement of wings. These butterflies love the twilight, when the owls also set out hunting. The small insect-eating vertebrates, particularly the small climbing mammals and bats also hunt at this time. All these creatures have a great respect for owls, and so are warned off by seeing the picture of the owl's eyes on the underside of a butterfly. The giant South American moth *Thysania agrippina*, which reaches the dimension of a vampire bat, brings fear and hesitation into the eyes of its pursuers when they see the design of the underside of its wings, which consists of black and white spots.

Not many observers notice that the Peacock Butterfly, when disturbed, gives out a rustling, grating sound, which is caused by sudden friction of its protruding forewing ribs against the backwing ribs. When the wings are fully expanded, the prominent peacock's eye becomes fully visible. This is not the only example of butterflies emitting rustling sounds, and other cases occur in South America.

Many Hawk-moths, such as the now almost extinct central European Spurge Hawk-moth and some of its relatives when they are disturbed have the habit of unfolding their wings sideways and spreading out the hind pair striped in pink and black, at the same time bobbing up and down on the ground in quick succession. Similar effective postures and movements are common in the most varied groups of Lepidoptera. Butterfly and moth collectors are familiar with the method of escape used by moths resting on grass. If the sleeping moth is not in a fit condition for instant flight, it will slip down in the grass, and using its feet will slide with a swift movement, deeper and deeper between the blades. It may even slide into a mouse hole, in order to give its pursuer the slip.

Most Lepidoptera are already protected in the egg stage. The individual eggs are generally glued by the females to various plants, and as their colouring is mostly green, they are almost invisible. Many species slide the eggs behind bark, into cracks in wood, into the axils of leaves and leaflets, buds and twigs. Many Tussock-moths and some Eggars cover the egg batch with a layer of hairs, which makes them nearly invisible. The rust-coloured hair covering of the eggs of the Gipsy moth mimics the wood-destroying polyporus fungus and is a superb camouflage for the 100 to 650 eggs which lie underneath. Such a hairy layer gives adequate protection to the overwintering caterpillars curled up inside the eggs; the rain slips over its surface and it insulates the batch of eggs.

The caterpillars of many Lepidoptera are usually well protected against insect-eaters. The most noticeable examples are in the family Geometridae, or the Looper moths, where the similarity of some caterpillars to twigs is quite remarkable. Many caterpillars of moths of the family Thyatiridae and the Sycamore moths resemble bird droppings. Other Sycamore moth species and all the Vapourer moths have their caterpillars beautifully and gaily coloured and the well-developed tufts of hairs safeguard them against most birds. The elongated hairs of some very small caterpillars of the Tussock moths spin fine 'spider's' threads which enable them to travel by air to a distance of tens of kilometres to new localities.

Head of a male specimen of the Emperor Moth (*Attacus edwardsii*) viewed from front

Scaly wing cover of the Lesser Emperor Moth (*Saturnia pavonia*)

The potently scented fork-like protuberance behind the head of the caterpillars of the Swallowtails (osmateria) are considered to be protective. In the case of many exotic Papilionids, the sides of the chubby fore-end of the caterpillar's body, which looks like a head, are decorated with vivid eyespots, whose design bears all the details of a real eye. The most exquisite example of this is the North American Swallowtail, *Papilio troilus*. The large eyespots, which seem to watch the observer, have all the characteristics of a real eye — the white surrounding the black pupils, the whitish shine and the expressive black borders. They glare at an intruder almost menacingly from within the caterpillar's sac-like shelter made of a leaf, just like the intently watching eyes of an unknown animal. The large caterpillars of some night-flying moths are sometimes equipped with strange, bizarre outgrowths, or bear snake-like designs with expressive markings which imitate the eye. An excellent example of this is the caterpillar of the east Australian Hawk-moth, *Coequosa triangularis*, which is green and covered with short spines, and whose front part of the body is turned into a lashing 'tail'. Its abdomen is turned into a 'ghost's head' with markings which mimic large glaring eyes.

The caterpillars of the Prominents, when attacked, defend themselves by raising the fore and hind parts of their body. Red, moving whips lash out from the fork-like end of the body, and a sharp liquid ejaculated from the holes under the caterpillar's head sprays the enemy. Many caterpillars also use various outgrowths on their skin as weapons of self-defence. The Fritillaries, for example, are equipped with forked thorns, many of the Emperor moths have feather-like growths, which, when touched, burn like nettles.

The pupae of Lepidoptera are usually well concealed in nature. When their time comes to pupate the caterpillars either bore their way into the earth, or hide in the leaf litter on the ground. They crawl into cracks and holes, under stones and behind the bark of trees. Less frequently they hang themselves on plants, or pupate in loose cocoons on various natural objects. The shape and coloration of the suspended pupae are usually adapted to their surrounding. Their colour actually forms according to the colour of their surroundings. The pupae, which stay hidden in the ground are more or less rounded, oval-shaped and without outgrowths. Sometimes they are encased in cocoons, or in fairly strong sheaths glued together from earth components.

The pupae which hang on plants are often presented in a bizarre form. They may look like thorns, or wood chippings, or their surface may be divided into ledges, spines, or other strange protuberances, which applies particularly to the Fritillaries. This can be most perfectly seen on *Cynthia arsinoe insularis*, a Fritillary from the island region of New Guinea. This species, when pupating, has on its dorsal side two rows of shining spots and two transverse ledges with lateral hooks, which resemble the wings of a bat. Many of the freely suspended pupae react to touch by a swift, whipping movement of the body, which can sometimes frighten a predator, but also sometimes attract his attention. The caterpillars of the Eggars, the Bombyx moths, the Emperor moths and some of the Prominents spin cocoons which are often very strong and in which the pupa is protected and almost completely safe. The caterpillars of some of the *Cucullia* moths spin covers from sand and stones for their underground pupation. It is difficult for an insect-eating animal to gnaw the way through the sandy sheath, spun together with a resilient silk thread.

Butterflies and moths are relatively well protected against larger enemies, but they fare badly when attacked by predatory insects. Particularly the parasites from the orders of hymenopterous and dipterous insects and the microscopic parasites cause immense losses to the Lepidoptera from time to time.

MAN'S IMPACT ON LEPIDOPTERA

We have seen in the previous chapter many examples of how excellently butterflies and moths are capable of protecting themselves against predators. These ingenious devices are really a result of natural selection operating through evolutionary time. This selection is governed by gradual, almost unnoticeable changes in the environment thus fitting the species closely to its surroundings. Insects have been in existence for more than 300 million years. About 250 million years ago winged insects first made an appearance but it was not until only 60 million years ago in the Cretaceous period of prehistoric time that the first butterflies and moths were seen. Their evolution has followed closely the evolution of the flowering plants on which they feed.

The rapid expansion of the world's industrialization in modern times has reduced the amount of natural vegetation available for wild life in general. Even so adaptations by the Lepidoptera to these new conditions are apparent. One of the well camouflaged European moths is the Peppered moth (*Biston betularia*). This moth has black and white mottled markings on the wings which make it virtually impossible to see on lichen covered tree trunks. Trees in industrial regions get coated in soot and are blackened. On such tree trunks the black and white mottled moth stands out and can easily be caught by predators, such as birds. A black mutation of *Biston betularia*, normally picked off lichen covered trees, has an advantage on sooty trees and it is protected from predators. Therefore today in industrial regions *Biston betularia* is almost totally represented by the all black or *carbonaria* form, while in the country, away from industry, the ordinary peppered form exists.

The continuing reduction in the natural vegetation together with the use of highly toxic pesticides have led to considerable reductions in the numbers of some insects in recent years. The delicate and sensitive butterflies and moths are particularly endangered. Through millions of years they have gradually adapted to the slow changes on the earth's surface but Man's activities may well be occurring at a rate faster than these insects can adapt. Some of the photographs in this book would be very difficult to take again as the species they show are much less common than they used to be. Careful use of insecticides in the future is needed to ensure that these rare species have a chance to increase again.

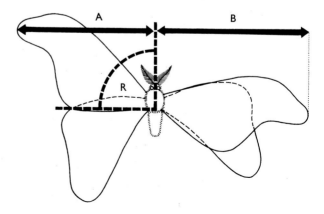

The left side of a butterfly, prepared according to international rules, shows the position of wings. The hind margin of the forewing and the longitudinal axis of the body form a right angle (R). In this position, abscissa A equals one half of the numerical value of the wingspan of forewings (Wsp) given in the marginal texts of this book. Abscissa B (always longer than A) indicates one half of the actual maximum wingspan which is not given in the texts. When measuring butterflies, prepared specimens almost always are used.

Many of the species which have survived through millions of years, are today extinct; they have disappeared from the landscape which decided not to spare them even a small patch of natural, uncultivated ground.

During the past two centuries, travellers have been importing butterflies and moths caught overseas into Europe, where the interest in them is ever growing — not only for scientific reasons, but also from the collector's point of view. Butterfly collecting is not always based on scientific interest and thirst for experiments. The beauty of butterflies has tempted Man into the manufacture of many kinds of souvenirs, made up either of the whole butterfly or only of the wings of the various vividly coloured species. Enthusiastic entomologists and their hired butterfly hunters carried on bringing supplies of the exotic butterflies to replenish the stocks of specialized companies. Butterflies and moths were caught in their hundreds, and their pupae and eggs were collected too. The market price was determined by the degree of their rarity — and was quoted in detailed indexes and sales catalogues. In the temperate zones entomologists collected species which, though not so vividly beautiful, were rare, and therefore valuable, in other countries. They often exchanged some of their specimens for other species, even for completely different collected objects. It was not an uncommon occurrence to find some unscrupulous entomologist clearing out a locality completely — which meant that a few years later certain species were absent from that particular habitat, or at best they became a rarity. This, however, was probably not the main reason why the very existence of butterflies and moths in cultivated countries has become massively jeopardized. The present situation, when many species — or, to be more precise, practically all species — are being reduced, was caused by the gradual destruction of their natural habitats which were vital for their development and adult existence. The species which inhabit forested areas have managed to survive in many localities, providing chemical controls were not applied in the forest industry of that particular area; but even here species abundance fluctuates so that for some period the species may be rare while at other times they become relatively abundant. Modern arable practice has reduced the stands of some wild plants to small localized patches. Butterflies and moths requiring one of these patchily distributed plant species either for food or to lay eggs on, have a harder job locating new plant stands. The countryside has been robbed of much beauty, of which butterflies and moths are an essential part. The sparse places of refuge, where some remains of the original cover of the Earth still remain are becoming gradually rarer, particularly in heavily populated areas where the demand for space is so great.

If the reader of this book, as he wanders through nature, still manages to find places which are butterflies' paradise, this should be an incentive to him and to all nature lovers to do their best to preserve everything that still can be preserved, so that future generations can still experience the pleasure of seeing a butterfly in flight over a meadow filled with colourful flowers.

Abbreviations used in marginal texts

Wsp – Wingspan of forewings
Fpl – Foodplant of caterpillar

Chapter 1   THE GUILD OF KNIGHTS   *Papilionidae*

The Swallowtails (Papilionidae) are some of the most beautiful butterflies, noted for their magnificent colours and elegant shapes. Some members of this family are equipped with ornamental 'spurs', like the privileged knights of the Middle Ages. The long spurs on the wings of the butterfly however often prove to be a snare for some pursuing enemy. During an attack the predator may seize this fairly unimportant part of the wing while the butterfly swiftly flies away.

The family Papilionidae contains more than 600 species of exclusively diurnal, heliophilous (sun-loving) butterflies, of medium to large size. Their wings are large, compact and rounded, with hind wings often concavely shaped on the inside and tapering to one or more spurs of varying width. The body, in comparison to the wings, is usually slight, the head is small, the eyes bare, and ocelli are absent. The legs are thin and long, with two claws on the feet. The front pair of legs is well developed in both sexes. The proboscis does not become stunted in the adult stage, but is always functional.

The caterpillars vary from hairless to spiny or even hairy but they all have a forked tubercle just behind their head, which is conspicuously coloured and has a pungent odour. This is called osmaterium. The pupae usually are supported with a girdle round their middle and are attached with their head facing upwards. Otherwise they lie on the ground in a thin web of silk; they are never suspended head downwards.

Scarce Swallowtail (3) is one of the most beautiful European butterflies, unequalled in appearance by many species of the tropics. It belongs to the butterflies which flutter and glide from early spring about the first flowering plants and shrubs. The Scarce Swallowtail used to be more common and its caterpillars were occasionally found even in gardens, but now it is increasingly rare. This is because in many parts of Europe people have destroyed blackthorn and hawthorn bushes, which are its natural habitat.

Iphiclides podalirius L.

Wsp ± 65 mm
Fpl Cherry, Plum, Sloe, Whitebeam, Hawthorn, Cotoneaster

1   2

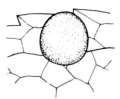

Egg of the Scarce Swallowtail

The caterpillars of the Scarce Swallowtail (1) are greenish, with reddish-brown spots. They live hidden in the leaves of blackthorn, hawthorn and other bushes and trees. The hibernating chrysalis (2) is coloured ochre to brownish-grey and secured by the cremaster and a tightly spun web to its base, head upwards. The cremaster is a small structure at the abdominal end of the chrysalis, equipped with a number of hooks, by which the body is attached to a silken pad spun by the caterpillar. From the cremaster experts can tell with the aid of a microscope the sex of the future butterfly.

4

Graphium sarpedon L. (4) lives in many geographical areas in the warmer regions of Asia,
especially in central and southern China and southern Japan. It is a most
beautiful butterfly, black with colourfully speckled stripes across both
wings. These specks form a semi-transparent band and are blue-green or
yellow. The hind wing is rimmed with a row of greenish half-moons.
The underside of the hind wings is decorated in red. Spurs are absent.
This Swallowtail is a swift flier, and never lingers long on garden bushes
or near the edge of woods when sucking nectar from flowers. Many
beautiful relatives of the genus *Graphium* which have wings similarly
prevalent with greenish-blue colours on black background, inhabit the
tropics of the Indo-Australian region and sultry Africa.

Wsp ± 60 mm
Fpl *Citrus*

27

The green caterpillar of *Graphium sarpedon* changes into a chrysalis approximately 33 mm long. The chrysalis (5) has a noticeably sharp protuberance on the upper side of the thorax and the surface of its body is roughly dimpled and green in colour. Yellow lines run horizontally from the tip of the thorax right along the body.

Papilio xuthus L. (6, 7) lives in the temperate zone of the Far East. Though slightly similar to the mid-European Common Swallowtail, its wing veins dividing the yellow areas have wider black borders, which give the wing greater variance of colour. There are also three horizontal black lines in the front area of the forewings. The underside of the hind wings is brighter too with orange and blue coloured eyespots. This butterfly is well known in China and Japan, where it likes to frequent the parks and gardens of large cities.

Wsp ± 100 mm
Fpl Citroideae

7

Papilio bianor Cr. (8, 9) is one of the so-called 'black' Swallowtails of exceptional beauty.

Wsp ± 110 mm
Fpl Citroideae

Mostly found in the tropical Indo-Malayan region, it also occurs in the Palaearctic parts of the Far East. *Papilio bianor* inhabits the zone stretching from southern China to the north, and the whole of east Asia as far as east Siberia. The two photographs here show the Japanese aberration: picture 8 a sitting female, picture 9 a mating pair of butterflies taken from above (the male is on top, the female underneath). The forewings of the male have patches of dark hairs, called scent-patches, used to attract the female.

Eastern Tiger Swallowtail (10) is one of the large Swallowtail species; it inhabits temperate
Papilio glaucus L.
regions of Canada as well as the central and eastern United States up to
Texas and Florida. The most interesting of its several forms demonstrates

Wsp ± 95 mm
Fpl Tulip tree, Birch, Cherry,
Plum, Ash, Lime, Willow,
Poplar, Whitebeam, Apple,
Sycamore, *Magnolia*

sexual dimorphism in colouring. Males of this more southerly form
(right) display a coloration unusual in Swallowtails — canary yellow and
velvety black with orange and blue markings on hind wings. Females
(left) are black-brown with rich blue and reddish designs on hind wings.

Pipe Vine Swallowtail (11 top, female) of the same family occurs in the eastern and southern
Battus philenor L.
United States. Its distribution area extends up to Nebraska in the west,
in the south as far as California. The dark brown basic colouring is

Wsp ± 75 mm
Fpl *Aristolochia, Asarum*
(*Polygonum*)

enhanced by rows of creamy white spots, hind wings and abdomen are
bordered with blue-green gloss. The underside of the hind wings bears
red-orange rounded dots and is edged with black and white half-moon
spots while the inner surface shines in blue-green. Margins are decorated
with sulphur yellow half-moon patterns, the base of the wings is dark
brown. The underside of forewings has a matt violet gloss.

**Pupa of the Pipe Vine
Swallowtail**

11

Black Swallowtail (11 left) is distributed east of the Rockies, from Canada to the south across
Papilio polyxenes Fab. Central America to the northern part of South America and occurs in
many diverse forms. The picture shows the race *P. p. asterius* Stoll from
Wsp ± 73 mm Ohio, USA, a sooty black Swallowtail with rows of egg-yellow spots.
Fpl Parsley, Caraway, The tips of its hind wings are decorated with blue curves and a reddish-
Daucaceae (e.g. Carrot) yellow eyespot with a black centre. The abdomen is dotted with yellow.

Zebra Swallowtail (11 right) is a Swallowtail of the genus *Eurytiaes*. It occurs in several seasonal
Eurytides marcellus Cr. forms. The basic coloration is brown-black, the wings are obliquely
striped with light yellow, almost white, bands. Its hind wings are en-
Wsp ± 67 mm hanced with vivid carmine spots and blue arcs at the tips. On the under-
Fpl *Asimina triloba,* side of hind wings several carmine spots are joined to form a scarlet band.
Annonaceae, Lauraceae, This species inhabits southern states of the USA from Texas to Florida
Heathers and to the north it occurs locally up to Canada. It develops only in
southern regions where the Paw-Paw tree grows.

Most of the dark coloured Swallowtails are distributed in the tropical
regions of the Far East. There are some magnificent butterflies among
them with extended hind wings, usually decorated with a white patch;

**Pupa of the Zebra
Swallowtail**

33

12

13

14

round the progressively concave hind wings they have large fiery-red spots.

Parides alcinous Klug is a Japanese species, which in some of its forms is most akin to the more southern, tropical beauties. Its larvae (12) are rather strange, studded with tubercles coloured red at the tip, and with greyish-white cross-stripes; this coloration serves to break up the uniform outline of the body. On the caterpillar pictured on the right, the protruding fork-like osmaterium is partly visible. All the Swallowtail larvae are equipped with such scent organs; when disturbed, they are able to push it out immediately. Perhaps the pungent smell emitted from this glandular organ protects the caterpillar against some of its enemies. *Parides alcinous*, as all other butterflies which inhabit the regions close to the Equator, has two or more seasonal generations, which often differ substantially in colour and size. Even the unusually shaped chrysalises of different generations are basically variable in colour. Picture 13 shows the pupa of the summer brood, picture 14 the pupa of the spring generation.

Wsp ± 80 mm
Fpl Aristolochiaceae

35

Eurytides leucaspis Godt. (15) has a large, yellow-green triangular patch on each open wing; their wide borders are yellow-brown and black and there is a red cross-stripe in front of the spur on the hind wings. The southern slopes of the Andes in Peru, Bolivia and the Ecuador are its main habitats. Males are more common; females, until recently unknown, stay hidden in the vicinity of their foodplants.

Wsp ± 85 mm

Atrophaneura coon Fab. (16) occurs mostly in the Sunda Islands. The illustrated butterfly from Java is black; the lighter patches on the hind wings are light brown, the two spots near the spurs are rich yellow. The narrow forewings, and the 'rudders' on the hind wings enable its swift gliding flight in the tops of tall trees, where it often resembles a black martin.

Wsp ± 115 mm
Fpl Lianas of the family Aristolochiaceae

16

17

18

19

Graphium doson Felder (18, 19) is wonderfully coloured both on the upperside and underside.
Wsp ± 60 mm
Fpl *Cinnamomum*
It is widely spread in many forms over a huge area of the Palaearctic and tropical Asia, from India and Sri Lanka, across Indo-China up to the Lesser Sundas. The pupa (17) adopts the colour of its surroundings.

Parides gundlachianus Felder (20) is one of the world's most beautiful Swallowtails. Though it is
Wsp ± 75 mm
Fpl *Aristolochiaceae*
often quoted as the most colourful of the American Swallowtails, it has, in fact, only four colours, similarly to many other American species. It is a Cuban endemite, inhabiting the southern and eastern rocky shores, but it can also be seen in the mountains, as high up as 1,000 m (Sierra Maestra). The male, as is apparent from the picture, has white patches of scent scales on its hind wings.

21

22

40

23

Graphium tynderaeus Fab. (21) can be found in the equatorial forests of western Africa. It is
black in colour, with rows of green, or yellow-green spots. The females
tend to be more yellow than the males. It is a swift flier.

Wsp ± 80 mm

In many parts of the world, particularly in the tropics, there are
Swallowtails which do not resemble the European types; they are more
likely to be identified with the species of the family Danaidae, or the
subfamily Heliconinae.

Papilio zagreus Dbldy. (22) resembles in colour and shape the two above-mentioned species.
There is no sign of spurs, the narrow wings are not developed and the
characteristic Swallowtail markings are absent too. Its colour is black,
yellow and reddish-brown. It inhabits the dark forests of Brazil, Peru,
Bolivia and the north up to Colombia.

Wsp ± 110 mm

Papilio alexanor Esp. (23) is somewhat similar to the Common Swallowtail, but its design is
different and its yellow colour is deeper. An excellent flier, it keeps
mainly to the mountainous districts and forest pastures, where it is
attracted by thistles. Small areas in southern France, southern Italy,
eastern Sicily, a few localities in Greece, also parts of Turkey, Caucasia
and Iraq, up to the south of central Asia, form its habitat.

Wsp ± 65 mm
Fpl Umbelliferae (*Ptichotis,
Seseli, Ferula*)

41

Fore part of a Swallowtail
caterpillar with protruding
osmaterium

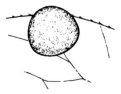

Egg of the Common
Swallowtail

Common Swallowtail (26) was at one time perhaps the most popular butterfly in Europe.
Papilio machaon L. Thanks to the destruction of the countryside and perhaps to the over-multiplying of parasites destroying its caterpillars and pupae, we know
Wsp ± 85 mm today this species mostly from pictures. The geographical distribution
Fpl Umbelliferae, of this butterfly is enormous. It occurred practically in all Europe, from
Ranunculaceae, Compositae, the south African shores to the North Cape and in the east, across the
Euphorbiaceae temperate northern Asia to the Bering Straits from where it spread into
North America up to Hudson Bay. Picture 24 shows the caterpillar of
this butterfly with the osmaterium fully exposed. Picture 25 portrays
pupae variably coloured according to their surroundings.

27

28

29

44

Graphium agamemnon L. (27) forms many geographical subspecies in the Indo-Malayan region. There are bright green spots and yellow stripes on the black-brown background of the wings. It may even occur in the vicinity of human habitations.

Wsp ± 65 mm
Fpl *Annona, Michelia, Saccopetalum*

Papilio nobilis Rogen. (28) is unusual in its colouring: the ochre yellow colour of the wings with the brown-black markings near the edges, changes in sunlight to a bright, extremely conspicuous yellow. It is found in West Africa. In the vicinity of Nairobi, the males are often caught by attracting them on dead butter-flies fastened to trees, or even on paper dummies.

Wsp ± 95 mm
Fpl *Wahlenbergia*

Druryeia antimachus Drury (29 — male) is the largest butterfly of Africa, inhabiting the humid forests in the west of this continent. Its colour is black-brown, with yellow, ochre and reddish markings. The long, narrow wings give grace to its gliding flight above woods, where the female butterfly leads its secret life; it is even today one of the greatest rarities of entomological collections. The male is illustrated here.

Wsp ± 230 mm
Fpl It seems to feed on a poisonous plant, for even the butterfly is strongly poisonous

30

The rich kingdom of beautiful Swallowtails in the Indo-Malayan
and Australian geographical areas includes perhaps the most exquisite
butterflies of the world. Many species, usually dark coloured, have
exceptionally elongated hind wings, which end in a long, spade-like spur
or are gradually tooth-edged, with beautiful colour markings. The forewings are decorated with deep, lengthwise grooves, which are made even
more conspicuous by their colouring: the rows of scales along the wing-
veins are light in colour against their black blackground. At one time
this Swallowtail group was named by the entomologist Haase 'the
grooved butterflies' — Rinnenfalter. These beautiful butterflies do
not occur solely in the purely tropical regions. A number of the Indo-

31

Malayan species spread into the adjoining areas of the Palaearctic region too, although this is otherwise the home of more sober butterfly forms. Such 'transitory' regions in·northern China and Japan are actually the habitats of the most beautiful species.

Papilio demetrius Cr. (30, 31) of Japan is one of them. The male, which is pictured here from above and below is darker on the upper side than other species. The female has red spots even on the upper side of the hind wings. Apart from Japan, this butterfly is also distributed in China and northern India. It flies from April to October in two generations. The larvae are green with a dark saddle and white spots on the sides of the body. They live on various citrus plants.

Wsp ± 120 mm
Fpl Citroideae

47

Papilio multicaudatus Kir. (32, male) is a North American Swallowtail coloured canary yellow and velvety black with blue and reddish markings at the tips of hind wings. It occurs in southwestern Canada and in the west of the USA across Montana and Nebraska to California and Colorado, in western Texas and to the south across Mexico to Central America.

Wsp ± 110 mm
Fpl Privet, *Ptelea*, Cherry, Plum, *Amelanchier*, Ash

Papilio agestor Gray (33) of Tibet is a butterfly surprisingly alike in shape, the faint
brownish-green colour and size to the inedible butterfly *Danaus tytia*,
and inhabits the same areas.

Wsp ± 90 mm

Graphium androcles Boisduval (34) is, in contrast to the two completely atypical species illustrated on the opposite page, a typical representative of its species. It is,
however, bigger than the well-known European Swallowtails and its spurs
are amazingly developed. Its black-brown, pale yellow and greenish-
yellow colouring is not very conspicuous, but as for the shape and size,
it is certainly one of the loveliest Swallowtails. An excellent flier and
glider, it is most difficult to capture; if caught, the fragile, extremely long
ornamental parts of the back wings nearly always break in the net. The
wooded river valleys of the Celebes Island are its natural habitat.

Wsp ± 85 mm

Swallowtails are one of the most gaily coloured butterflies we know.
The wealth of their colours is particularly apparent when they are seen
in larger groups.

34

Atrophaneura polyeuctes Dbldy. (35 — female from below), from Taiwan, has its hind wings decorated with white and red spots. It occurs also in the Himalayas, in Bhutan and on the Malayan Peninsula.

Wsp ± 115 mm

Papilio krischna Moore (36) occurs in Sikkim and Bhutan. It is a magnificent butterfly of the mountains, whose dark wings appear as if sprinkled with glittering greenish scales. Other colours — violet-blue, yellow, green and red — adorn the hind wings. It inhabits mountain meadows and edges of forests up to the altitude of 3,000 m.

Wsp ± 90 mm

Parides bolivar Hew. (37 — male), a beautiful creature of the South American virgin forests, lives along the upper reaches of the Amazon and Orinoco Rivers.

Wsp ± 75 mm

Papilio karna carnatus Rothsch. (38) from northern Borneo is one of the 'moss green' butterflies — it is 'sprinkled' with green scales. The hind wings have a blue flame-like pattern, violet-brown eye and a green band. Considered a jewel of the south Asian fauna, it is a precious item in any collection.

Wsp ± 100 mm

Papilio blumei Bsd. (39) is one of the most beautiful and biggest of Swallowtails. The wide band of its wings turns from blue-green to violet-blue. Northern Celebes is its habitat. When gliding above water, it sometimes touches its surface in the same manner as swallows do.

Wsp ± 110 mm

In tropical South America Swallowtails without spurs and mostly with dark-coloured wings prevail. The wings, however, are often decorated with white, green and red patches, which may even have a rich opalescent sheen; sometimes the greenish-blue coloration turns into scarlet.

Pachliopta hector L. (40) occurs in India. Though the forewings are most unusually coloured, the two rows of blood-red spots on the hind wings are the most conspicuous. It is abundant from the lowlands to the giant mountains and is known for spending the nights gregariously in trees.

Wsp ± 80 mm
Fpl *Aristolochia*

It is difficult to tell which family or group of butterflies is the most beautiful; quite often, however, the large Swallowtails from the tropical eastern Asia and the island region of New Guinea and Australia, the so-called *Ornithoptera*, head the list. They have stood in the centre of man's interest from the time of their discovery during the big collecting expeditions overseas; the big, and mostly wonderfully coloured butterflies were then named after the heroes from the Greek mythology and after the queens of the great maritime powers. The travellers could hardly fail to notice the big, dark, robust butterflies, which fluttered around the tops of the tallest trees or glided over the water, not unlike strange, glittering birds, according to which feature they were named *Ornithoptera* — birdwings. Some of the species were paid for with gold, others were used as royal gifts and many of them — now almost extinct — are today protected by law and are among the greatest and the most prized treasures of some zoological collections. About a half of the total number of these Swallowtails is variously coloured, frequently with magnificent shimmer-

41

42

ing gold-yellow, green, violet and blue patches. The females are usually more sober in colour — black-brown with dirty grey-brown spots. The other half consists of black butterflies, whose hind wings are decorated with bright yellow patches. The males do not differ much from the females. Generally, the females of most *Ornithoptera* are far bigger than the males, being ones of the largest existing butterflies.

Troides helena hephaestus Felder (41 — male) from Celebes is one of the black-coloured members of the group. Its caterpillars feed on plants of the genus *Aristolochia*.

Wsp ± 125 mm

Ornithoptera paradisea Stgr. (42 — male) is unique in the shape of its hind wings. The colouring is black, gold-green and yoke-yellow, and it occurs on New Guinea. The female, which is always bigger than the male, is inconspicuously coloured in shades of black-brown with grey-white spots; the hind wings are rounded, without spurs.

Wsp ± 120 mm – male
Fpl *Aristolochia*

Ornithoptera victoriae Gray ssp. **reginae** Salvin (43 — female) from the Solomon Islands. The photographed specimen measured 165 mm; in some other races the females may measure up to 220 mm when the forewings are fully extended. The male is black and magnificently gold-green.

Fpl *Aristolochiaceae*

53

44
45

Ornithoptera priamus L. ssp. **urvillianus** Guérin (44 — male) from the Solomon Islands. Wingspan of its forewings is about 140 mm.

Ornithoptera croesus Wallace ssp. **lydius** Felder (45 — male) from the islands around New Guinea is another highly prized butterfly species. *Aristolochia* sp. are foodplants of its caterpillar, the same as in preceding species.

Wsp ± 150 mm

Troides aeacus Felder (46) from Taiwan and the surrounding areas is the only *Ornithoptera* species to penetrate into the Palaearctic region.

Wsp ± 95 mm

Ornithoptera priamus L. ssp. **poseidon** Dbldy. (47 — male), a magnificent green form, inhabits New Guinea and the Moluccas.

Wsp ± 150 mm – male

Those who will never have the opportunity of seeing these fairy-tale creatures alive, can only imagine how wonderful they must look in flight.

47
46

Trogonoptera brookianus Wallace (48) is an excellent flier with slender wings. It often leaves the virgin forest and likes to sit near paths in the vicinity of human habitations. Whole swarms of these butterflies can frequently be seen feasting there upon rubbish heaps. Sumatra, Borneo and Malaysia are its main habitats. The female is less colourful than the male, but is far rarer.

Wsp ± 150 mm – male

Festoons, Apollos and a few other, mutually related butterfly species also belong to the family Papilionidae. They inhabit mainly the Palae-arctic region; some occur in tropical Asia. Of these all, only the Apollo occurs also in North America. These beautiful butterflies belong to the thermophilous (warmth loving) species, although the Apollo keeps mostly to the slopes of high mountains. The majority of them inhabit the Mediterranean region and places further to the east; the occurrence in central Europe is very rare.

Caterpillar of an *Ornithoptera* **species**

Southern Festoon (49) is yellow with black markings, blood-red dots and blue arches. Southern
Parnalius polyxena Moravia and southern Slovakia form the northern boundary of the
Denis et Schiff distribution area of this lovely butterfly. Until recently it was fairly
abundant in its habitats, but it is getting more and more rare nowadays.
Wsp ± 55 mm The idyllic vineyards, where its foodplant, *Aristolochia*, grew as a weed,
Fpl *Aristolochia clematitis* were turned into prosperous vineyards and all weeds were destroyed and
excluded. At the same time, in the damp lowland forests where *Aristo-
lochia* still survives, the natural biotopes are changed by artificial regula-
tion and the butterfly disappeared due to the application of insecticides
against mosquitoes. In places where the Southern Festoon has managed
to survive, it may be seen flying from early spring, at the end of April
and in May.

Central Asia Festoon (50) is a straw yellow butterfly with black markings. Each forewing bears
Hypermnestra helios a red, black-rimmed spot. This butterfly appears only in one generation
Nick. which can be seen flying in spring. Green caterpillars pupate in a loose
cocoon in the ground where they also hibernate. They feed on plants of
Wsp ± 45 mm the genus *Zygophyllum*.

Luehdorfia japonica Leech (51, 53) is a related species from Japan, but it resembles more the
true Swallowtails. This wonderfully coloured butterfly appears in the
Wsp ± 60 mm early spring, in mid-April, when there is still snow in the mountains.
Fpl Aristolochiaceae It may be seen fluttering mainly round the plants of the family Compositae and violets, and is not difficult to catch. After fertilization, the

51

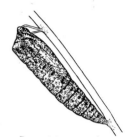

Caterpillar of the Southern
Festoon before pupating

Pupa of the Southern
Festoon

52

53

females have a protective scale-like organ (sphragis) below the end of the body, which feature can be also observed in the Apollo females. The hairy, brown-black caterpillar (52) lives mostly on asarabacca plants. It hides during the day among stones under plants, which is also the place where it pupates. When reared in captivity in Europe, the caterpillar may be fed with the European *Asarum* species, *Asarum europaeum*.

Bhutanitis lidderdalii Atk. (54) is a beautiful, exotic relative of the Festoons. This breathtakingly lovely, precious butterfly lives in the eastern part of the Himalayas, in Bhutan and the adjoining Assam, also in a locality in Burma.

Wsp ± 105 mm

54

Its slightly varied form is known from neighbouring China. Mountains and mountain valleys, where tall trees are still growing, are its natural habitat, for it likes to flutter about in their crowns. The naturalists, who were fortunate enough to reach these wild and inaccessible regions to study this butterfly, report that on a windy day it resembles a dry leaf being carried by the wind. When the butterfly is resting, it hides all the beauty of the hind wings under the forewings, which makes it inconspicuous. Observers also say that the living butterfly has a most pleasant smell which even lingers on for some time after it dies. Caterpillars feed on lianas of the family Aristolochiaceae.

59

55

56

60

Teinopalpus imperialis Hope (55 — female) is a relative of the preceding butterfly and has
a similar range of distribution. Generally, it is coloured green, grey-violet
Wsp ± 85 mm
Fpl *Daphne*
and yellow. The colouring of the male is more vivid and more yellow
than that of the female, which is far less common. The female is also the
bigger of the two, and has on its hind wings three antler-like spurs
instead of the one of the male. This mountain-dwelling butterfly is
a swift and skilled flier.

Archon apollinus Herbst. (56) is found in the east Mediterranean region in Greece, Bulgaria,
and in Turkey, and in the east as far as Armenia and south to Lebanon.
Wsp ± 50 mm
Fpl *Aristolochia*
It is grey-brown, with yellow patches and black and red markings. It
occurs in several forms in sunny places in very early spring.

Parnassius autocrator Avinov (57, female) from the Hindu Kush mountain range Chodja
Mohamed has large, bright orange kidney-shaped spots on the hind
Wsp ± 65 mm
Fpl *Corydalis ideantifolia*
wings.

The Apollos are butterflies of medium size, and the Palaearctic region
is their original habitat. As a rule they are whitish or yellowish, with
striking black veins and black or red spots on the wings.

The subfamily Parnassiinae has a wealth of subspecies and races,
reaching up to several hundred forms. They are usually very rare, and
quite difficult to catch in the inaccessible mountainous regions which
generally form their habitat.

57

58

59

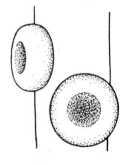

Eggs of the *Parnassius apollo*

Parnassius nomion Hbn. ssp. **richthofeni** O.B.H. (58, female) is probably the most beautiful
representative of its family, with its rich wing decoration of large, red
eyespots. This butterfly occurs in the heart of China, in the wildest parts
of the Nan Shan mountain range, northeast of Lake Ching-Hai.

Wsp ± 60 mm

Parnassius apollo L. (60) inhabits Spain, the mountainous regions of the Pyrenees, the Alps,
Corsica, the Balkan mountain range, the Carpathians, parts of Scandi-
navia, the Caucasus and regions further to the east. The photographs
show a female of the Carpathian subspecies *P. apollo carpathicus* Reb.
Rog. from the eastern part of the Low Tatra. The caterpillar is shown
on picture 59. Artificially bred caterpillars can be fed lettuce leaves.

Wsp ± 80 mm
Fpl *Sedum telephium,*
S. carpathicum, S. album

60

Between both polar circles of the Earth, over the most inhospitable giant mountains and into parched steppe regions, stretches the distribution area of representatives of the family Pieridae — the Whites. It comprises about one and a half thousand species, most of which are coloured white or yellow. However, we may occasionally come across a beautiful White coloured orange or red, and there are in fact even Whites in which the black colouring prevails. These butterflies are mostly of a medium size, and the inner borders of their hind wings are convex-shaped. The two sexes usually differ in colour. The caterpillars are often thickly covered with short hair, and their body is narrowed at both ends; the head is small and spherical. The pupae, similar to those of the Swallowtails, are suspended head upwards and secured with a silk girdle. The crown of the head is frequently pointed.

Brimstone (61) is perhaps the most popular of all the mid-European Whites. The male's colour
Gonepteryx rhamni L.   is canary yellow, the female's a pale yellow-green. This attractive and
harmless butterfly is widespread throughout all the Palaearctic region
Wsp ± 55 mm   of the Earth, with the exception of Arctic countries and some islands.
Fpl *Rhamnus*   In central Europe it is one of the most welcomed and one of the first

61

heralds of spring; often it will fly from its winter shelter into the country-side where some snow still remains. It deposits its eggs singly in buck-thorn bushes, which later become the abode of the green caterpillar. In summer the caterpillar changes into an unusually shaped pupa (62). The butterfly hatches during summer, and in winter hibernates hidden in bushes and dry leaves.

Berger's Clouded Yellow (65) was discovered and described by R. Verity in 1911. It is the most
Colias australis Verity interesting of the mid-European species. For a long time it was mistaken
for the similar Pale Clouded Yellow — *Colias hyale* L., which today

Wsp ± 45 mm
Fpl Crown Vetch, Horseshoe
Vetch

**Egg of the Berger's Clouded
Yellow**

survives only in the regions rich in the original wild vegetation. The Pale
Clouded Yellow is a known roamer, and at times it is even described as
a migrating butterfly, whereas Berger's Clouded Yellow never leaves its
native locality, where it can be found flying from May till autumn. It
inhabits southern Europe and the more temperate parts of central Europe
and Asia up to the Caucasus. Its caterpillar (64) can be distinguished
from the green caterpillar of the Pale Clouded Yellow by the rows of
black spots. The pupa (63) is green, with sharp lateral edges and a slightly
convex-shaped thorax. In our picture the markings of the future butterfly
are slightly apparent.

65

Orange Tip (64, male) occurs in southern and central Europe, spreading even far into the north.

Anthocharis
cardamines L.

Wsp ± 40 mm
Fpl Garlic, Cuckoo Flower,
Alyssum, Barbarea, Thlaspi

The genus *Anthocharis* inhabits the whole Palaearctic region of Eurasia and North America. The most vividly coloured species are found in the Mediterranean and in North Africa.

In April, when the cuckoo flowers are in blossom, the Orange Tip likes to rest on them. The female lays eggs on various cruciferous plants, especially on the garlic mustard. The caterpillar (67) which is blue-green in colour with a sharply defined grey-white stripe along the body, is fond of nibbling the young pods of the garlic mustard, which also serve as an excellent hiding place for it.

Egg of the Orange Tip

67

The pupa of this attractive butterfly (68) is very interesting. It weathers the winter suspended by the end of its body and by a thin girdle on a dry stalk somewhere in bushes near the water's edge, which is the place where its foodplants, the garlic mustard and bittercress, usually grow.

68

Pupa of the Cloudless Sulphur

Caterpillar of the Cloudless Sulphur

In order to escape the attention of insect-eating birds, which in winter search the bushes for anything eatable, the pupa develops such a shape that it has to a certain extent the hope of survival till spring; it resembles a greyish-brown thorn and is therefore able, on a thorny bush, to deceive even the sharp birds' eyes.

Cloudless Sulphur
Phoebis sennae L.

Wsp ± 60 mm
Fpl *Cassia, Trifolium, Viciales*

(69, below, female) makes its home almost everywhere in North and South America. Males are usually lemon yellow while females are darker, rather rusty coloured with a greater number of rusty-brown markings on their wings.

Sleepy Orange
Eurema nicippe Cr.

Wsp ± 40 mm
Fpl *Cassia, Trifolium, Viciales, Chamaecrista*

(69 above) is one of smaller American species. It flies in the northeastern part of the United States in the vicinity of the Great Lakes, as far west as Nebraska, and south as far as Brazil. Its shiny orange-yellow wings are bordered with a broad brown-black band.

69

72

In the warm Central America several Yellows of the genus *Meganostoma* occur, which are also locally called 'the dog's head'.

Meganostoma eurydice Bsd. (70, male) from California, has markings on the forewings which resemble heads taken from the side. The underside of the wings strongly resembles the European species of the genus *Colias*. The caterpillars, covered with short hair, are blue-green in colour with small black dots.

Wsp ± 53 mm
Fpl *Amorpha californica*

Hebomoia glaucippe L. (71) the largest White of the world, is at home in the tropic regions of India, Sri Lanka, south China, the Sunda Islands and on many of the small islands scattered in this region. The females do not wander far from their foodplants, but the males form whole swarms which gather on the wet, sandy shores of rivers and brooks. When the wings are closed, these butterflies resemble dry leaves.

Wsp ± 90 mm
Fpl Climbing lianas
(Capparidaceae)

Delias harpalyce Don. (72) from south Australia occurs from early spring, which, in this part of the world, starts at the beginning of October. The caterpillars live gregariously high in the crowns of trees, and they also pupate in groups.

Wsp ± 65 mm
Fpl Loranthaceae

71

There are many species of butterflies which undertake long journeys like migrating birds. Some of the best known travellers come from the family Danaidae, which consists of nearly 1,000 species of interesting medium and large-sized butterflies which inhabit the warmer regions. Their wings are always smooth-edged, without spurs, and the males have well developed scent glands. The caterpillars are gaily coloured and appear bald, with non-retractile protuberances on the thoracic and tail segments. The pupae often are a beautiful gold, with a robust body which is narrowed in the middle; they are suspended head downwards by the cremaster.

Idea leuconoe clara Esch. (73) from Taiwan is one of the largest representatives of this family.
Wsp ± 120 mm   It is coloured black and white.

Pteronymia cotyto Guérin (74) from Central America has black markings on its transparent wings.
Wsp ± 45 mm

Lycorea halia Hbn. (75) from southern Brazil has wings coloured black, ochre and reddish-brown.
Wsp ± 80 mm

73

Pupa of the Monarch

74

Caterpillar of the American Monarch

Monarchs sleeping gregariously in trees

Monarch (76) from Central and Southern America is the most popular of all Danaidae species.
Danaus plexippus L.   Each year after hatching in spring it travels to the north. The butterflies fly through the American states in clouds numbering millions of specimens, and penetrate as far as Canada. Occasionally specimens blown off course may reach western Europe. With the approach of autumn, these magnificent travellers return to the south again. During the journey they spend the nights gregariously in trees, and it is interesting to note that they always choose the same ones they rested upon during their spring migration.

Wsp ± 80 mm
Fpl Asclepiadaceae

74

Chapter 4   THE LARGE FAMILY OF NYMPHALIDS   *Nymphalidae*

The family Nymphalidae includes the best known, the most colourful and therefore the most popular butterflies. Their distribution over the earth is enormous, as they occur in all continents where the weather conditions are favourable. Today there are over one and a half thousand known species, and new ones are still being described. They are light-loving, diurnal butterflies of medium to large size and usually gaily coloured. The caterpillars are either slug-shaped with the bald body tapering at the rear end, or they are covered with rows of hard, branching protrusions. They pupate in loose pupae which are sometimes decorated with horns and other protrusions on their surface, and always hang head downwards. Frequently they have silver or golden patches.

Some tropical species are among the most colourful butterflies. There are, however, a great number of inconspicuous, dull-coloured species living in the tropics, some of which have even developed 'invisible' forms. On the other hand, areas with moderate or cooler climate, are surprisingly enough, the habitat of some of the most colourful and beautiful members of this family.

Peacock Butterfly (77) is one such example. It has a most unusual wing design with 'peacock
Inachis io L.   eye' marks on each wing, which is unique among all butterflies. All southern and central Europe are its habitat, from the British Isles east-
Wsp ± 55 mm   wards to Asia and further still to Japan. Along the whole area of its
Fpl Nettle, Hop   distribution it even penetrates far into the north, almost to the Arctic Circle.

77

78   79   80

The caterpillars of the Peacock Butterfly (78) are black, spiny, with white spots; they live gregariously on nettles and on hop and pupate into a slender, golden chrysalis (79). Its colouring is grey-brown or green, according to the colour of the surroundings at the time of pupation. In the south they have two generations, in the north only one. The butterflies hibernate in shelters.

Painted Lady (80) has
Vanessa cardui L.

Wsp ± 55 mm
Fpl Compositae, Boraginaceae, Viciaceae

similarly vast distribution area as the Peacock Butterfly. Furthermore it inhabits all Africa, and spreads further north in Europe, and occurs also throughout Asia including tropical Indo-Australia. It lives even in North America, but it is not very common there. It is a beautiful butterfly, with the upperside of wings coloured pink and yellow-red and dotted with black and white spots.

Pupa of the Painted Lady

Caterpillar of the Tawny Emperor

76

Tawny Emperor (81 above left, male), a Nymphalid of North America, belongs to the Apaturidae. The males' wings lack gloss and iridescence. It occurs in the belt from New York to Nebraska, to the south up to Texas and to the east as far as Florida. Its upper surface is light yellow-brown with white and dark, almost black, dots.

Asterocampa clyton
Boisd. et Lex.

Wsp ± 45 mm
Fpl *Celtis occidentalis*

Aglais milberti Godt. (81 below left) is a true North American Nymphalid, in appearance and mode of life very much like the European Small Tortoiseshell. In contrast to the latter, this species has very dark central wing areas which are brown-black, sharply defined against outer margins. It inhabits Canada from the Pacific coast to Newfoundland and spreads to the southwest to western Virginia and to the west to California.

Wsp ± 45 mm
Fpl Nettle, Willow,
Helianthella, Asterales

Goatweed Butterfly (81 above right) inhabits the region stretching from the Great Lakes to Texas with the exception of southern Florida. The genus *Anaea*, occurring mainly in the tropical part of South America, is classified in the subfamily Charaxinae. The pictured male, originating from Texas is coloured a cloudy orange with darker, brown wing borders. The female of this race has lighter wings with conspicuous, dark brown design.

Anaea andria Scudder

Wsp ± 55 mm
Fpl *Croton capitatus,*
C. monanthogynus

Doxocopa lavinia Butler (81 below right) is one of the most typical American Nymphalids, called 'Buckeye'. Several of its aberrations occur from southern Canada to the south as far as tropical South America. It is grey-brown in colour, with dark ochre bands along outer wing margins. Forewings display two stripes of the same colour and eight peacock eyespots which may be coloured black, blue, violet or light brown.

Wsp ± 50 mm
Fpl *Linaria, Gerardia, Sedum,*
Lippia, Verbena

81

Pupa of the 'Buckeye'

82

Camberwell Beauty (82, 124) is also widely distributed. It occurs in Europe, Asia and America,
Nymphalis antiopa L. preferring regions with deciduous forests both in the lowlands and
mountains. In the vicinity of brooks and gardens it can sometimes be
Wsp ± 65 mm seen sucking sap from injured trees. The Camberwell Beauty hibernates
Fpl Birch, Poplar, Elm in a sheltered place, appearing in the early spring, and a second time
in the autumn. Unfortunately it seems to be continually decreasing in
number. The larvae live gregariously.

Comma Butterfly (83) is found throughout Europe including the Mediterranean regions, and
Polygonia c-album L. further to the east across Asia to Japan. Several similar, related species
live in North America. The Comma Butterfly is easily recognizable by
Wsp ± 45 mm its toothed wing-margins and the white design in the shape of the letter
Fpl Red and Black Currant, 'C' on the underside of the hind wings. It hibernates and appears in the
Gooseberry, Nettle, Elm early spring and in summer.

84

False Comma (84, 85) occurs in eastern Europe and southwards to Japan, also in North America.
Nymphalis vau-album On the rusty-white wings it has four white dots, and on the underside
Denis et Schiff. of the hind wings a white letter 'L' (85).

Wsp ± 60 mm
Fpl Willow, Elm, Birch

85

Yellow-legged Tortoiseshell (86) is a rare Euro-Siberian species. It can be distinguished from the Small Tortoiseshell by its larger size. The edges of forewings bear a pale, almost white, spot. Caterpillars feed on willow.

Nymphalis xanthomelas Schiff.

Wsp ± 60 mm

Large Tortoiseshell (87 — pupa) is more abundant in its Euro-Siberian homes. This beautiful butterfly which used to adorn the trunks in summer alleys, has now become rare enough. Caterpillar foodplants are elm, poplar and willow.

Nymphalis polychloros L.

Wsp ± 60 mm

89

Small Tortoiseshell (89, 123) is a Euro-Siberian butterfly, widespread in all Europe; to the
Aglais urticae L. north it penetrates as far as Cape North, and its eastern area of distribution covers the whole of Asia up to the Pacific Ocean. In North America
Wsp ± 47 mm the Small Tortoiseshell is replaced by the similar species *Aglais milberti*
Fpl Nettle Godt. After leaving its winter shelter, which is often a cellar or attic, the
Small Tortoiseshell occurs on the first flowers of the spring, mainly the
sallow, daphne and crocuses. Often it can be seen flying through the
streets of the busiest parts of a big town. The spiky caterpillars, decorated
with yellow lateral stripes, live gregariously on nettles.

Red Admiral (90, 91) inhabits Europe and the adjoining parts of Asia, northern Africa and
Vanessa atalanta L. North America and penetrates as far south as the Isthmus of Panama.
This magnificent vagrant can often be seen during its long journey in
Wsp ± 55 mm the late summer as it feasts upon fallen pears together with bees and
Fpl Nettle bumblebees. If left undisturbed, it will stay in such places for several
days. Picture 88 shows the pupa.

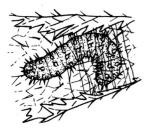

Caterpillar of the Red
Admiral in a twisted nettle
leaf

92

After the warm days of summer, the cool, damp days of autumn come to the temperate zones. The butterflies of the last Red Admiral generations crawl into cracks, under bridges, or into other dark corners, where

93   94

they hope to weather the winter (92). Very few Red Admirals, however, survive till the spring. The arrival of new immigrants from the warm south in the following year preserves the population of this species in the northern regions. Picture 93 shows a Red Admiral trapped behind a windowpane.

Polygonia c-album L. ssp. **hutchinsoni** Robs. (94) is an interesting form of the Comma Butter-fly, originated from the first spring generation, of which only about 30 % individuals hatch. It looks like a specimen of a different species. The colours are paler and the wings less concave. Also the underside of the wing is a light ochre instead of the dark brown-green. The caterpillars pupate in crevices and cracks of old wooden fences, walls, window ledges, etc. The pupa (95) has well-defined colours.

Wsp ± 45 mm
Fpl Nettle, Elm, Willow, Hop

Map Butterfly (96 — 99) is the smallest palaearctic member of the family Nymphalidae and also one
Araschnia levana L. of the prettiest. A Euro-Siberian species, it lives in deciduous woods. This
butterfly is an excellent example of seasonal variability. The two genera-
Wsp ± 35 mm tions, hatched in different seasons of the year, are so unlike that we may
Fpl Nettle easily take them as two completely unrelated species. No wonder, therefore, that they were often described and named differently. In the tropics
there are many such cases — for instance the African Nymphalid *Precis
octavia* Cramer is a dark blue during the dry season, but red in the rainy
season: the generation which appears between these two is partly blue,

97

98

and partly red. Such changes bring not only pleasure, but often also troubles and worry to the entomologists. Pictures 96 and 98 show the summer form of the Map Butterfly (f. *prorsa*), whilst pictures 97 and 99 illustrate the spring form (f. *levana*), hatched from a hibernating pupa.

99

Brood of the Map Butterfly on the underside of a nettle leaf

100

101

Anaea marthesia Cr. ssp. **confluens** Stgr. (100), the yellow coloured form from the virgin forests of the lower reaches of the Amazon River is reddish-brown on the upperside with shimmering yellow-brown patches on the wings. The underside (102) is a colourful symphony of brown, grey-black and violet shades.

Wsp ± 70 mm
Fpl Samydaceae

Anaea fabius Cr. (101) from South America, has a faint marble-like pattern on the underside.

Wsp ± 75 mm
Fpl Piper marginatum

The tropical genus *Hypolimnas* of the family Nymphalidae, widespread throughout the Indo-Australian and African regions, contains usually large, striking, black butterflies with blue and yellow-brown markings on the wings.

102

Hypolimnas dexithea Hew. (103), the largest of this genus, inhabits the forests of northern and eastern parts of Madagascar.

Wsp ± 93 mm

The African species are often coloured a conspicuous blue. Some others imitate the grey-brown colouring, the size and the arrangement of wing spots of butterflies of the family Danaidae, which the insect-eating vertebrates find inedible. Other beautiful and interesting Nymphalids are members of the genus *Hamadryas* (*Ageronia*) which live in Central and South America from the Yucatan Peninsula southwards to Paraguay. Most of them have inconspicuous grey colouring, interrupted by a fine pattern, but there are also species which are magnificently coloured.

Hamadryas arethusa Cr. (104 — female), is velvety black from the upper side with glossy blue

Wsp ± 70 mm
spots, so that it looks as if studded with diamonds. The males have scent scales in the centre of their hind wings to attract the females. The *Hamadryas* genus — butterflies of mostly medium size, are agile fliers which react quickly to their surroundings. When disturbed during feasting on the sweet sap escaping from the bark of trees injured by beetle larvae, they quickly fly away. When in flight their wings make unusual rustling noise.

The European Nymphalids do not have their back wings decorated with spurs. Only the Comma Butterfly has tooth-edged wings and the *Charaxes* species from southern Europe has two short protrusions. In the tropics, however, Nymphalids with spurs do exist — such as the genus *Marpesia* from South America, and the genus *Salamis* from Africa.

The South American species
Marpesia coresia **manifests
the division of the under
wing surface in resting
position**

107

Ruddy Dagger Wing (105) from Mexico is vividly reddish-brown on the upper side with black-
Marpesia petreus
Cramer
brown streaks; the underside is inconspicuously greyish-brown with
a violet sheen. A continuous dark stripe runs across the underside of
both wings, resembling the primary vein of a leaf, with the spur imitating
Wsp ± 80 mm
Fpl *Anacardium*
the petiole. This butterfly flies sometimes from the tropical South America to the southern United States.

Salamis anacardii duprei Vins. (107) lives in Madagascar. The wings are black and white,
faintly bluish, with an opalising iridescent sheen. The red eyespots on the
Wsp ± 80 mm
Fpl *Anacardium*
hind wings are bordered with yellow and red. The underside of the
wings (106) is a pale ochre-white, and the pattern resembling the veining
of a dry leaf is visible when the butterfly is resting.

93

108

Among the butterflies of the tropical countries, there are hundreds and thousands of examples of the excellent adaptability of colour and shape to the surroundings. The dull, inconspicuous colours of the under-wings provide protection when the butterfly is resting. When in flight, it does not need such protection, and therefore the upper sides of the wings may be vividly and gaily coloured.

Anaea archidona Hew. ssp. **magnifica** Fruhst. (108) from the virgin forests of Colombia has the underside of its wings similar to the patterns of an ancient pharaoh's cloak embroidered with silver. Even here is it possible to recognize in this strange design the vein structure of a dead leaf which was lying for some time on damp ground. The silvery patches give the illusion of holes caused by some insects and small molluscs, or of dew or rain drops. The main 'primary vein', a dark line which, when the wings are

Wsp the larger form
± 100 mm, the normal form
A. archidona Hew. ± 90 mm

94

closed, runs through the centre of the underside, is found again and again not only in related species, but also in species which in their development are completely different. When examining a specimen in a collection, we can see that both its sides are symmetrical; and symmetry is always conspicuous in nature. Nevertheless, it looks quite different when resting among dry leaves.

Anaea archidona and particularly its larger form, *magnifica*, is a very rare butterfly, a pride of any collection. In this species even the upper side (109) is relatively inconspicuous. When in flight, the butterfly resembles a dry leaf carried by the wind. It is worth noting mostly because of its elegantly shaped wing margins and the simplicity of its coloration and design. We cannot mistake this butterfly for any other species. The females are usually larger than the males, with duller colouring and a less distinct wing pattern.

109

Historis odius Fab. ssp. **orion** Fab. (111) inhabits South and Central America; it is velvety black-brown, with rusty patches on the forewings, which are further-more decorated in their front part with a drop-like white spot; the hind wings have yellow-brown margins. The underside (110) is tobacco-brown. This robust butterfly is well known throughout its native countries, for it likes to flutter about villages, sucking the remnants of food and over-ripe fruit, or the sap from injured trees.

Wsp ± 100 mm
Fpl Cecropia peltata

Cyrestis thyodamas Boisduval (112) lives on Taiwan, in China and in the East Indies. It is a nacreous white with variously coloured veins and bands distantly resembling a cracked stone.

Wsp ± 50 mm
Fpl Fig

Several species of the extremely beautiful 'leaf butterflies' of the genus *Kallima* occur in the Indo-Malayan region, and some others also in Africa. The upperside of the forewings has a wide, light band, coloured according to the actual species — brown-orange, greenish, red or violet.

97

Kallima inachus Boisduval ssp. **formosana** Fruhst. (113) represents the subspecies from the Island of Formosa (Taiwan). The underside of the wing is in picture 114. *Kallima inachus* occurs in many forms in India, in the temperate regions of China and on nearby islands.

Wsp ± 73 mm
Fpl Acanthaceae

Zaretis isidora Cr. (115 — underside of female) from Colombia, resembles a decayed leaf, when at rest.

Wsp ± 60 mm
Fpl *Casearia*

Members of the genus *Cethosia* are distributed through the Sunda Islands in Melanesia. Of medium size, they slightly resemble the Fritillaries and the Nymphalids. Their colour design is strikingly complicated.

114

A *Kallima* species sitting on a twig resembles a leaf

115

116

Cethosia gabinia Weym. (116 — female) is black and white with an iridescent sheen and in the centre of the hind wings has a colour design composed of bluish-grey, yellow and black. The females are prettier than the rusty red males. The Island Nias, west of Sumatra, is their habitat.

Wsp ± 70 mm
Fpl Passifloraceae (e.g. Passion Flower)

South America is the home of some one hundred species and several hundred subspecies and forms of an interesting type of butterflies. Their wings are narrow and long, usually rounded at the tip; they are slow, but persistent fliers, and like to glide from flower to flower. They spend the night in groups on branches of bushes and trees. These are Heliconidae, which were formerly classified as a subfamily of Nymphalidae, but now, according to the opinion of experts, are considered an independent family. They fly lazily, displaying their vivid colours, for they have no reason to hide. They happen to be repulsive to birds and to other insect-eating animals.

The greatest part of American Heliconids inhabit tropical regions. Only a small number of species spread to the subtropical and temperate zones. Species illustrated here are most abundant in North America.

Philaethria dido L. (117) come s from South America (Brazil, Peru) and is blue-green with black-brown borders. Caterpillars feed on plants of the family Passifloraceae.

Wsp ± 83 mm

Gulf Fritillary (118 left) occurs from Argentina to the United States south of the Great Lakes. Its upper surface is orange-brown with black markings while the underside bears silvery nacreous spots. Caterpillars feed on *Passiflora* sp.

Agraulis vanillae L.
Wsp ± 60 mm

Zebra Butterfly (118 right) inhabits southeastern United States round the Gulf of Mexico, the Antilles and tropical South America. Its velvety black upperside bears sulphur yellow transverse stripes.

Heliconius charitonius L.

Wsp ± 80 mm
Fpl Various species of the genus *Passiflora*

The large South American Nymphalids of two mutually related genera, *Prepona* and *Agrias* are extremely strong and persistent fliers, with their

The underside of the Gulf
Fritillary

117

Pupa of the Gulf Fritillary

119

thoracic muscles particularly well developed. If trapped in a net, they put up a hard fight for their life. They are too lovely to go unnoticed, and as many of them are very rare, they are valuable also commercially. They can be lured to the forest margin by the smell of fruit and the stench of offal, or even of faeces and carrion. They are very fond of feeding on all this, as well as on the sap of wounded trees, and though they are extremely wary and cautious, they will return again and again to such snares. The members of the genus *Prepona* have their forewings cut in the shape of a scythe. The underside is inconspicuously grey-brown with a faint dry-leaf pattern.

Prepona demophon L. ssp. **muson** Fruhst. (119) from Colombia has black wings with blue bands, which have often a greenish or violet sheen.

Wsp ± 95 mm
Fpl *Mollinedia laurina*

Prepona praeneste Hew. (120 — male) from Colombia and Peru, is an example of the red and blue coloured species. The males have scent tufts on the hind wings, which are used to attract the females. The fiery colours and the rich lustre of the wings cannot be expressed by a mere photograph.

Wsp ± 90 mm
Fpl Annonaceae

In the warmer parts of the Palaearctic and in the tropical Indo-Australian region, Nymphalids of the genus *Euthalia* occur. They are coloured an inconspicuous brown or green with light dots.

Euthalia dunya Dbldy. (121) from Java is brown with a greenish underside; the spots on the wings are yellowish-green.

Wsp ± 80 mm
Fpl Ebenaceae, Myrtaceae

103

121

122

123

Precis almana L. (122) the pluvial-period form is rusty brown above and pale yellow on the
underside, with a dry-leaf design. The Indo-Malayan region, including
the Sunda Islands, China and Japan, is where this butterfly occurs

Wsp ± 86 mm
Fpl Acanthaceae

Small Tortoiseshell (123) (see text on page 82 and picture 89) and
Aglais urticae L.
Camberwell Beauty (124) (see text on page 79 and picture 82) are shown in their natural
Nymphalis antiopa L. surroundings.

The butterflies of the genus *Agrias* belong to the most exquisite jewels
of South American nature. In contrast to the *Prepona* species, they have
very gay patterns on the underside of the wings which often resemble
beautiful works of embroidery.

**Pupa of the Camberwell
Beauty**

124

105

Agrias narcissus Stgr. (125 above — the male with scent tufts) comes from the Amazon region. [125]

Wsp ± 67 mm

Agrias claudina Godt. (125 below — underside of the male) is from Peru.

Wsp ± 80 mm

A great number of medium- and small-sized and often very beautiful Nymphalids live in the tropical zone of America. The underside of members of the genus *Perisama* is usually more soberly coloured, whereas the *Catagramma* and *Diaethria* species, which occur at higher elevations, often have very vivid coloration on their underwings. In some the designs resemble various numerals.

126

Catagramma excelsior pastazza Stgr. (126 top left — underside of wings) lives in Ecuador and Peru.

Catagramma codomannus Guérin (126, top right — underside of wings) occurs in Colombia and Brazil.

Diaethria anna Guérin (126, centre left — the underside; centre right — the upperside) is
Wsp ± 40 mm   from Mexico.

Catagramma peristera Hew. (126, bottom right — the underside) is from Brazil.

The tropical Africa, Indo-Malayan region and, to some extent, even the Palaearctic region, are the home of some robust Nymphalids which in colour and beauty equal the butterfly jewels of South America.

Charaxes jasius L. (127) has brown wings with a light yellow-red border; the hind wings are decorated with a row of blue spots and have two short spurs each. The underside of the wings (127 above) is much gayer in colour and richer in design. It is considered as one of the most beautiful European

Wsp ± 75 mm
Fpl Strawberry Tree

butterflies and may be found in the narrow belt along the coast of the Mediterranean Sea; two subspecies are found in tropical Africa.

Butterflies of the *Polyura* genus usually have a large light area on both sides of their wings, but the decoration round this yellow or greenish patch is uniquely neat.

Polyura eudamippus formosanus Rothsch. (128 — male) has its yellow-green wings rimmed with a black-brown border; the hind wings have a yellow and a blue-grey dot by each spur. Several exquisite and rare subspecies inhabit various countries of the Indian subcontinent and Malaya. The males seek elevated places where they stay on the look-out for the females.

Wsp ± 65 mm

Equatorial Africa is the home of butterflies of the genus *Charaxes*. Over seventy species of these magnificent butterflies of all possible colours and most unique designs inhabit the regions of the humid forests and also the dryer bush-covered savannas. All shades of blue, red, yellow, brown and green may be seen on the wings of individual species.

128

129

Charaxes castor Cr. (129, underside of wings) is one of the largest members of the genus.
Across its wings spreads a wide yellow-brown stripe, which disintegrates
into spots on the forewings. The hind margin of the underwings is
decorated with a row of blue spots. As in most members of this genus,
the underside is more interesting. They live on the sap from wounded
trees, but also suck on decaying fruit, excrement or refuse. The hairless
caterpillar which has horns on its head and body covered with tubercles
lives on tropical woody plants.

Wsp ± 100 mm
Fpl *Tragia, Afzelia, Sorghum*

Baeotus baeotus Dbldy et Hew. ssp. **deucalion** Felder. (130, the underside). This species, found
in Colombia, Ecuador and the Amazon Basin, is similar in appearance
Wsp ± 80 mm to some species belonging to the genus *Charaxes*. Although unrelated,
these two genera share the same dispersed pattern on the underside of
the wings, a large head and a robust but short body.

In central Europe, where the forms of life developed less lavishly than
in the tropics, it is mostly the Admirals and the Emperors which remind
us of the beauty of the tropical butterflies.

131

Poplar Admiral (131, male) is the largest of these. The wing underside comprises two basic,
Limenitis populi L. contrasting colours: the ochre yellow-red is covered with pearly blue-grey
dots. The hind wings are decorated with a stripe divided by veins, and
Wsp ± 75 mm the inner side round the abdomen has an opalescent sheen. The outer
Fpl Aspen borders of the wing also have shining blue-grey rims with black and
white half-moons. The female (133) is larger than the male and, when
viewed from above, displays a more definite white pattern. The row of
orange coloured half-moons along the back border of the wings is also

132

133

more conspicuous and is followed by a succession of grey-blue stripes, which are invisible in the grey colouring of the male. The butterfly is at home in the greater part of central Europe, in Sweden and Finland — practically up to the polar circle; its eastern area of distribution covers the whole of Asia to Japan. Natural, mixed forests are its favourite habitats, especially in the vicinity of brooks and rivers. This is also where the caterpillars can be found, mostly on aspens. In the autumn, the small caterpillar spins a winter cocoon (hibernaculum) on a thin twig, in which, partly hidden, it spends the winter (132). The winter cocoon is almost impossible to find in the aspen undergrowth. Barely one centimetre long, it is tied with the threads closely to the twig. After the hibernation, the caterpillar feeds on the sprouting aspen leaves (134); during May it is ready to pupate. Then it spins a web and attaches itself to an aspen leaf, and changes into a chrysalis (136) which is about 27 mm long. To discover a pupa, suspended at a height of several metres from a leaf,

134

is one of the greatest thrills of a collector, who also needs experience
and luck on his side. The butterflies start to hatch in June and they fly
till the end of July. They leave the pupa in the morning. The males
flutter and glide over woodland paths, or stay near the edge of a forest,
or on pastures. They prefer higher altitudes — submountainous regions,
or mountain dells. Rarely do they rest on tree-trunks, woodland paths or
stumps, and then only in the morning (135). Sometimes the Poplar
Admirals can be found on fresh dung or carrion — which may make
a suitable bait if we want to attract them. As the day's warmth intensifies,
they climb higher into the crowns of tall trees, descending only when
wanting to suck the sap from injured bark, or to drink from a well or
a pool. In central Europe this butterfly occurs only in those localities
where the forest is left undisturbed and where foresters are not cutting
down the aspen and the sallow growths, which are considered as weed
in woods.

136

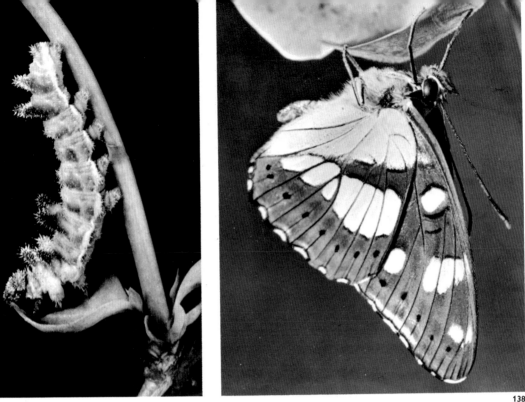

137

138

Southern White Admiral (138 — underside of wings) occurs in the warmer parts of Europe — *Limenitis reducta* Stgr. Spain, western France, Italy, Greece and the Mediterranean islands — and further north across the Caucasus as far as Persia. It is a relatively **Wsp** ± 50 mm rare species; in central Europe it can be found sporadically only in **Fpl** Honeysuckle southern Slovakia, which forms the northernmost boundary of its area of distribution. In warmer regions it ascends from the lowlands high up into the mountains. Its velvety black wings, which have a beautiful bluish sheen in living specimens, are decorated with a white band and white spots. The outer margins of the forewings bear a row of blue dots. The large light patch at the base of the hind wings is grey-blue in colour with a nacreous sheen, and a row of black dots runs along the outer hind wing margin. The green caterpillar (137) is covered with fleshy, reddish warty outgrowths of a various length, which are equipped with short bristles. The character of these outgrowths is quite different in the case of the White Admiral caterpillar, as in this species they are narrow and pointed and have long black spines.

American White Admiral (139 left) is similar in appearance to many Palaearctic Admirals. Its *Limenitis arthemis* upper surface is black-brown with a white band and rows of blue arcs Drury along wing margins. The underside is lighter and more vividly coloured. Except for a white band, similar to that of the upper side, a red-brown **Wsp** ± 60 mm ground colour prevails. This species is bound to deciduous groves and **Fpl** Poplar, Willow, Birch, their immediate vicinity. It inhabits southern Canada and northwestern Hawthorn, *Amelanchier* United States.

116

California Sister (139 right, male) is another species of North American Admirals. Its dark
Adelpha (Limenitis) brown upper colouring bears an oblique white stripe which disintegrates
bredowii Geyer on the forewing. In the fore corner of the forewings there is a large
ochre spot, in the hind corner of the hind wing a small one. The butter-

Wsp ± 65 mm fly's underside is splendidly coloured in white, black, brown, ochre,
Fpl *Quercus chrysolepis* red-ochre and sky-blue with play of colours. This species of the American
west inhabits California, Arizona, New Mexico, southwestern Colorado,
western Texas and extends across Mexico as far south as Guatemala.

139

White Admiral (140, the upper side of wings) is very gaily coloured on the underside of its wings.
Limenitis camilla L. On the other hand, the upper side is brown with a wide white band across both wings, which on the forewings disintegrates into dots. This species
Wsp ± 55 mm is absent in southern and northern Europe, occurring eastwards across
Fpl Honeysuckle Central Asia as far as Japan. The two rows of black spots on the outer margin of the hind wing underside serve as a good distinguishing feature when compared with the preceding species. A lover of damp, wooded valleys with brooks and rocks, it likes to sit in sunlit places on the ground, or on bramble flowers. The pupa (141), which is suspended either from the underside of a honeysuckle leaf or from a twig, is one of the loveliest to be found in the temperate zone.

Young caterpillar of the White Admiral on a bitten basis of a honeysuckle leaf which it later twists and spins with fibres

The Emperors are even more beautifully coloured than the Admirals. They are excellent fliers and are similarly built as the most skilled, exotic fliers of the genera *Prepona*, *Agrias* and *Charaxes*: they have a large head, a powerful, muscular thorax and a very small abdomen. Even the larvae of the Emperors resemble the larvae of their exotic relatives; they have an unusual shape, a rough skin and they are uncommonly agile. Also the habit of keeping in the vicinity of their food-plant and of returning to the same spot is shared by all these species.

119

142

Lesser Purple Emperor (142) has the upper sides of the wings shaded in red; the forewings *Apatura ilia* Schiff. are decorated with a clearly marked eyespot and the underside of the hind wings is violet-yellowish-brown, without the white band. The **Wsp** ± 60 mm butterflies fly in July and August in damp, but warm valleys with **Fpl** Aspen, Black Poplar deciduous woods.

The caterpillar of the Lesser Purple Emperor — *Apatura ilia* is quite identical to that of *Aparatura iris* except that the horns are coloured black in front. Both these Emperors have a similar geographical distribution, which runs through central Europe to the east across Asia and up to Japan.

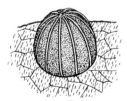

Egg of the Purple Emperor

Picture 143 shows the caterpillar of the Purple Emperor — *Apatura iris*. It is greenish, bluish on the underside, and has yellow grains and stripes on its skin. The bluish head is equipped with two long horns, which are red at the tips.

120

Purple Emperor (145) is dark brown with white dots and a white stripe. The wings have a magnifi-
Apatura iris L.

Wsp ± 63 mm
Fpl Great Sallow, Eared Sallow

cent blue sheen. The underside of the hind wings is decorated with a wide, pinkish-white band (146). The pupa (144) is green.

The small family Libytheidae is usually classified close to the Nym-phalidae family. This family embraces about 10 species whose many aberrations, however, occur in all continents. For American species, the new generic name *Libytheana* has been recently introduced, contrary to the Old World genus *Libythea*.

146

147

Snout Butterfly (147 above) is an American species, whose upper side is dark brown with ochre
Libytheana bachmanii
Kirt.
smudges in the central wing areas. The tips of forewings display four whitish dots. This migratory species is distributed practically throughout all of the United States, mainly in more southerly regions up to Mexico.

Wsp ± 45 mm
Fpl *Celtis occidentalis,*
Symphoricarpus occidentalis

The Meliteinae are usually classified as a group of the Nymphalidae family. They are mostly tiny butterflies, very variable in colouring, similar in appearance to the Fritillaries, coloured mostly rusty brown.

Chalcedony Checkerspot (147 left, female) is one of the largest of these butterflies. The upper
Euphydryas chalcedona
Dbldy et Hew.
side of its wings bears yellow dots on black-brown background while the margins and centres of forewings have red-brown spots. This species comes from California, Arizona, Nevada and Oregon. Caterpillars feed

Wsp ± 50 mm
on honeysuckle and plants of the families Scrophulariaceae and Dipsacaceae.

Pathed Butterfly (147 right, male) is one of the tiny species. The illustrated specimen from
Chlosyne lacinia Geyer
Texas is coloured black-brown with rusty-white stripes and dots on the wings. Its many generations fly in the area from southern United States

Wsp ± 40 mm
Fpl *Asterales, Xanthium*
to Argentina.

124

Small Silver-bordered Fritillary (148 left). Related types of these small Fritillaries are distributed mainly in Palaearctic Europe and Asia, a small number of species live in North America. The upper side of its wings is vividly red-brown with black markings and dots while the underside is partly red-brown, partly ochre yellow. It inhabits subarctic Canada including Alaska, Labrador and Newfoundland and can be also found in more southerly regions of the United States, in the central USA only in mountains. It also lives in north Europe and Asia, extending as far as the Polar Circle.

Clossiana selene Schiff.

Wsp ± 37 mm
Fpl Violet, Cranberry, Wortleberry, Bilberry, Strawberry

Great Spangled Fritillary (148 right) is one of the largest and most beautiful American Fritillaries. Its upper surface is coloured a vivid brown-orange with black dots, arcs and spots. The wing halves near the base are darker, black-brown, dusted in scales of the same colour as the rest of the wings. It inhabits the southeastern part of Canada and the USA from North Carolina and Georgia to California in the west.

Speyeria cybele Fab.

Wsp ± 80 mm
Fpl Violaceae

148

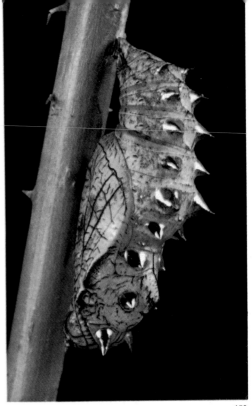

149

150

151

Childrena childreni Gray (151) is from Tibet. The silvery bands and spots on the underside of

Wsp ± 80 mm
Fpl Violet

its hind wings seem too conspicuous to give protection to the butterfly when it sits with the wings closed. But if we study the coloration of the front parts of the upper wings, it becomes evident that it matches the colour of the hind pair. When the butterfly is at rest, the striking red patch disappears and only the green area, broken by the bands, is visible.

The Fritillaries are true jewels of the mixed forests of the temperate zone.

Marbled Fritillary (152, 158) is a subspecies of the Argynninae Fritillaries. It flies in June and
Brenthis daphne Schiff. July in forest clearings and dry hillsides overgrown with blackberry or

Wsp ± 45 mm
Fpl Blackberry, Raspberry,
Bramble, Violet

wild raspberry bushes, where it likes to sit on the flowers. Southern Europe including Sicily and the warmer regions stretching eastwards to Japan are this butterfly's habitat. From southern Europe its distribution area reaches across Hungary and Austria to Slovakia.

Several hundreds of the Fritillary species, together with the similar subfamily of Meliteinae occur mainly in the Palaearctic region, less abundantly in North America and very rarely in the mountains of Africa and the Indo-Australian region. They are mostly of medium or small

152

153

sizes, usually rusty reddish-brown with black dots on the upper side and often with nacreous patches or bands below particularly on the hind wings.

The caterpillars of the Fritillaries have thorny tubercles, just like true Nymphalids. The well-fed, adult caterpillar attaches itself by the end of its body and hangs head down. It remains in this position without moving many hours, and changes into a pupa on the second or the third day. The thin skin behind the head cracks, and a new skin appears underneath; with the aid of slow contractions the old skin is pulled to the lower end of the body. The new pupa is at first quite soft, shapeless,

154

155

indefinitely green, resembling a sack filled with liquid. It takes many hours before the pupa gains its definite colour, shape and hardness, which guarantees a certain degree of security. The pupae of the Fritillaries, like the caterpillars, closely resemble the Nymphalid pupae. On the dorsal side of the abdomen they often have gold-coloured, cone-shaped protuberances. Picture 149 represents the adult caterpillar, picture 150 the pupa of the Marbled Fritillary.

Silver-washed Fritillary (153, 154 — female) is the largest of the central European Fritillaries.
Argynnis paphia L. It is distributed throughout central Europe and northwards to 63°N and from here to the east through the wooded regions of Asia to Japan. It

Wsp ± 60 mm
Fpl Violet, *Rubus* is rusty red on the upper side, while the underside (155) is greenish, interspersed with glossy, opalescent stripes, which are white in colour with a pinkish shade. The butterflies fly in July and August in one generation. The caterpillars, like all other central European caterpillars of the Fritillaries, hibernate.

129

156

157

The dark pupa of the Silver-washed Fritillary (156) adapts its coloration to that of the bark of pine trees, from which it is often suspended.

Sometimes it may be found low above the ground, in the vicinity of violet growths, on which the caterpillar originally lived. The dorsal side, under the thorax, is decorated with low cone-shaped outgrowths which have a steel-blue sheen.

Dark Green Fritillary
Mesoacidalia aglaja L.

Wsp ± 50 mm
Fpl Violet, Snake Root

(157) is another jewel of the European woods. Similarly to the preceding species, it can be most often found in forest clearings, but is also fond of woodland meadows. It is slightly smaller, but equally beautiful. The hind wings are decorated with rounded, pearly spots. It is more abundant in woods and is distributed throughout Europe, including most of the islands, and penetrates far over the Arctic Circle to the Northern Cape in Norway. To the east, its area of distribution stretches over suitable localities in Asia and China as far as Japan. In central Europe this butterfly flies from June to August. The caterpillar hibernates and pupates in June.

Many Fritillaries have the underside of their hind wings beautifully marked and coloured, but without the typical nacreous spots. These are also absent on the wings of *Melitaea* butterflies and other related genera. The Marbled Fritillary (158) — see also picture 152 — is another butterfly which lacks the nacreous spots on the wing underside.

Chapter 5 THE BLUE JEWELS OF THE FOREST *Morphidae*

With an amazing persistence and graceful ease the large, iridescent members of the family Morphidae circle above the crowns of trees. These 'spirits of the forest' do not frequently descend to the ground. Perhaps they are tempted only by sandy river banks, where they like to quench their thirst and gather strength for further flight. Man takes advantage of this knowledge and traps them there, using moving coloured rags, mirrors, or paper butterfly dummies as bait.

The family Morphidae comprises about 100 species of diurnal heliophilous butterflies, usually of a substantial size. Their body is comparatively slender and small, but the wings are large; the male's upper side mostly has a glittering sheen and the underside is decorated with rows of round eyespots. When viewed from the side, the thorax is deep and the abdomen small. The caterpillars live gregariously in nests on dicotyledonous plants. They are slender, of a cylindrical shape, narrowed towards the end; they are gaily coloured and have tufts of hairs on the dorsal side of the body. The head is relatively large, equipped with two horns pointing forward. The pupae are short but thick and egg-shaped, and suspended head down; they have two short horns on the head. They are usually yellow or green.

159

160

Morpho menelaus L. ssp. **tenuilimbatus** Fruhst. (159 — male) from Brazil, is azure-blue.
Wsp ± 130 mm   The underside is a mat brown, marked with silvery dots and a row of
large circular discs.

Morpho hecuba L. (160) from Guyana, is one of the largest of this family and has eyespots on
Wsp ± 145 to 250 mm   the underside of the wings.

Morpho sulkowskyi Kollar (161) from Colombia has an unusual pearly colouring. The fine
Wsp ± 83 mm   design of the underside is visible through the partly translucent wings.

133

161

162

Morpho didius Hopffer (162), the largest of the blue-coloured species, often falls a victim to the collectors. The female is brown on the upper side, with blue stripes and white dots along the wing margins. It lives mainly in Peru and in the adjoining regions of Colombia.

Wsp ± 165 mm

Morpho catenaria Perry (163, 164) has a chain-like row of brown eyespots on the pale blue-green background. The Morphos of this type usually have the coloration of the upperside and the underside more or less the same. On the other hand, the opalescent blue Morphos have their undersides mostly inconspicuously coloured, often with rows of eyespots.

Wsp ± 95 mm

The Morphos are excellent fliers and the males especially are extremely wary. Because of their spectacular colouring and the attractive sheen of the wings, they have always been much sought after by the hunters.

Pupa of a *Morpho* species

Ages ago the Indians caught them for ritual purposes. The wings were used for making masks for religious dances, amulets and ornaments. Later, when exotic souvenirs were very much in fashion in Europe, the wings of the Morphos were used in the making of 'artistic' pictures, in decorating trays, bowls and other similar objects. Today this species is no more threatened by the danger of extinction. It is protected by law and it seems that the South American forest has ample supplies to provide for the hunters of the future, who would catch this butterfly purely for scientific and collection purposes.

The densely hairy caterpillars, with a large head and gaily coloured body which thickens in the middle, live in communal cocoons in trees until the time of pupation. At night they crawl out in search of food, then return again to their spun homes. They live mainly on creeping lianas. Their hairs are rather brittle and break easily; if handled, they

165

can cause an irritation of the skin similar to that caused by *Porthesia* and *Thaumetopoea* caterpillars.

Morpho rhetenor Cr. (165, 166 — male), is one of the opalescent blue Morphos, but the underside of the wing is a perfect imitation of a dry leaf. The wings are divided into irregularly shaped areas coloured in various shades of brown, with a reddish hue. This species lives in northern Brazil and in Guyana.

Wsp ± 120 mm

The male of *Morpho rhetenor* (166) is metallic blue. Towards the margins of the wings the blue colour is darker, with a violet shade. When the wings are turned from side to side, their centres have a greenish-blue hue. The female is mat, red-brown on the upper side, with black-brown borders. It is substantially larger than the male.

When describing the Lepidoptera of the South American forest, one must not forget the family Brassolidae — butterflies of a medium size, often very robust and striking in appearance. Both the Morphidae and

137

Brassolidae families share many features and characteristics with the Browns of the family Satyridae, which are also well known in Europe. Of the two, the Brassolidae are even more related to them in the shape and habits of their caterpillars. The largest and the most interesting of the Brassolidae are the so-called 'owl butterflies', especially those of the *Caligo* genus. These are very large, attractive butterflies. Their coloration, too, is unique. Many have on the upper sides the iridescent deep blue shades of the Morphos, and the males also have the scent scales, located on the wings close to the abdomen.

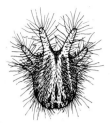

The owl butterflies (*Caligo*) are interesting not only because of their giant size, the opalescence of their surface colour, but also because of the large 'owl eyes' which are the striking feature of the underside of their wings. When disturbed, the butterfly will expose the two huge 'owl-eyes' to its enemy so suddenly, that it must often have quite a startling effect, especially when it starts to flutter its wings. This seems to be a good defence against small insect-eating animals, which themselves often fall prey to an owl. It is also interesting to note that these butterflies fly mainly at dusk and in the dark.

Head of a caterpillar of
a *Caligo* species viewed from
front

168

Caligo eurilochus Cr. (168) inhabits Honduras, Surinam and Guyana.

Wsp ± 138 mm
Fpl Banana

The Indo-Australian region is the home of a substantial number of butterfly species of the family Amathusiidae. They are also very closely related to the Satyridae and to the South American Morphos, resembling them in size and coloration. The underside of their wings is gaily coloured and the upper wings are often sheeny blue.

Stichophthalma howqua Westw. ssp. **formosana** Fruhst. (169) is found in Taiwan. Unlike
the blue species it is ochre yellow-brown with black arrow-shaped spots
Wsp ± 100 mm by the outer wing margins. Several geographical races occur in the subtropical region of China and along the Gulf of Tonkin. It flies early
in spring.

170

Caligo atreus Kollar ssp. **uranus** H. Scharff. (167, 170) from Honduras has its large wings coloured mostly dark brown with a blue iridescence; a wide, ochre border decorates the hind wings. The underside (170), on the other hand, has a very fine colour design. When this butterfly is disturbed during daytime, it will fly over to a nearby tree or into dry leaves and settle again with its head downwards, so usually it manages to merge with its surroundings. It is similarly difficult to spot when feasting upon the sap escaping from injured trees.

Wsp ± 115 mm
Fpl Musaceae, Bamboo

Butterflies of the family Amathusiidae from southern Asia have a similar way of life to that of the family Brassolidae from southern America. They too fly only short distances in the wood during daytime, being most active at dusk and in the dark.

Stichophthalma camadeva Westw. ssp. **camadevoides** Nicev. (171 — the underside) from Sikkim and Burma, has a glossy blue-green upper side with dark brown spots, and therefore resembles the American Morphos. Also the underside of wings is similar: it is decorated with eyespots and slanting lines.

Wsp ± 100 mm
Fpl Monocotyledonae, Palmaceae

171

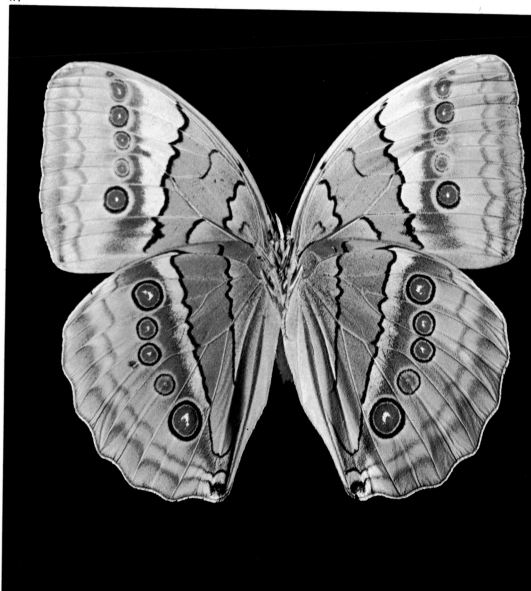

143

In suitable localities of all continents, both in lowlands and highlands, there occur many inconspicuous butterflies, which have one thing in common: small eyespots on their wings. These are the Browns, or the family Satyridae, which is one of the largest of all butterfly families. The eyespots on their wings are not striking, and therefore can hardly have any frightening effect. It is much more probable that their design divides the surface of the wings and so the attention of a pursuing enemy is usually transferred to another, less important part of the butterfly's body. The Browns, small or medium-sized butterflies, are particularly fond of twilight and shade. Their colouring is quite inconspicuous; the brown colour is presented in various shades, from the lightest ochre to almost black. But there are also Browns with red, blue, green and metallic colours, or even white, transparent and marbled ones. Their wings are mostly rounded, and the veins on the forewings are usually swollen at their base. The round-headed caterpillars are almost bald and taper towards the tail end; they are coloured brown to greenish usually with longitudinal stripes. The last segment of their body is forked. They feed on monocotyledonous plants. The pupae are barrel-shaped, with two protrusions on the head. They may be usually found lying on the ground, either freely or in a loose cocoon. North America is the home of many species of Satyrids very similar to those known from the northern hemisphere of the Old World.

Wood Nymph (173 above) closely resembles the Palaearctic species. The upper wing surface
Cercyonis pegala Fab. is brown-grey, forewings bear a more or less marked ochre-yellow spot.
In males, the centre of this spot forms a blackish blue, yellow-bordered
Wsp ± 55 mm eyespot with a white dot, females possess two eyespots. Many varieties
Fpl Grasses of this species inhabit the area extending from central Canada to Mexico.

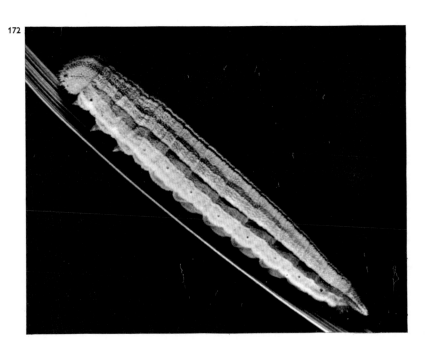
172

173

173 a

145

174

Ringlet (173 below) is one of the small species. This butterfly of a circumpolar distribution
Coenonympha tullia inhabits almost all of the USA (occurring in many local varieties) and
Müller cooler areas of Europe and Asia up to beyond the northern Polar Circle.
Its upper surface is ochre brown with eyespots from the underside
Wsp ± 36 mm showing through. The underside is more gaily coloured, fore and hind
Fpl Grasses wings being more differentiated. Forewings are a vivid ochre, hind wings
olive brown with whitish markings.

Marbled White (174, 175) flies in the temperate and southern parts of Europe from the end of
Melanargia galathea L. June to August. It also inhabits the Atlas Mountains in North Africa
and in the east occurs throughout Asia Minor beyond the Caucasus.
Wsp ± 50 mm
Fpl Grasses
It is mostly fond of hilly regions, particularly if composed of limestone.
In agriculturally developed regions with extensive fields this species now
occurs only at the edge of woods, and in woodland meadows and pastures.
At one time it was quite abundant on hillside meadows and rocky knolls,
but these are now disappearing due to changes in land use.

The female of the Marbled White, which is slightly larger than the
male, probably drops its eggs in flight into grass, or on various plants.
The eggs are smaller than 1 mm — they measure, in fact, 0.96 mm.
Picture 172 shows the caterpillar, picture 173a the pupa of the European
Marbled White.

175

Chapter 7   BLUES, HAIRSTREAKS AND SKIPPERS   *Lycaenidae*

If the Blues of the family Lycaenidae were three times their size, they would surely be considered the most beautiful among butterflies. It we examine a Blue with a magnifying glass, we can see similar glitter, play of light and coloration as on the wings of the South American Morphos. And what beauty we see when we observe various species of the tropical Hairstreaks! From the three thousand known species we are only able to show here a few meagre examples.

The Blues occur in all the continents, but they are most abundant in Africa and South America. They are diurnal, heliophilous butterflies, generally of a small size. The hind wings often have spur-like outgrowths. The larvae are usually flattened from the underside and convex-shaped on the back, with short hairs, short feet and a retractile head. They live a secret life, quite often in the company of ants. The pupae are short and roundish, immobile and frequently hairy. They either lie loose, or are tied with a girdle head upwards; in some other species, however, the pupae are suspended by cremaster head downwards.

Theritas (Evenus) coronata Hew. (176 — male) from equatorial and Central America is one of the largest Blues; it is shiny blue-green on the upper side, and on **Wsp ± 58 mm** the undersides has a red-violet band on the green-dusted background. The females also have two scarlet spots on the upper side of their hind 176   wings.

177

178

179

White-letter Hairstreak (177) flies from the end of June till August in woodland rises of central
Strymondia w-album
Knoch.
Wsp ± 30 mm
Fpl Elm, Oak, Lime, Alder
Europe and from there spreads eastwards up to Japan. Though dull brown in colour, the underside of the hind wings has a white, zig-zag line resembling the letter W, and an orange band on its outer side.

Black Hairstreak (178) resembles the preceding species, but the underside of its hind wings
Strymondia pruni L.

Wsp ± 30 mm
Fpl Blackthorn, Plum
has a row of black, silver-rimmed circular spots inside an orange-coloured bow-shaped patch. It also has similar distribution to White-letter Hairstreak and is fond of dry, bush-covered and rocky slopes, where it likes to fly in the vicinity of blackthorn thickets. The caterpillar is inclined towards cannibalism, which is not unique in the Lycaenidae family.

Copper (179) has the hind wings bluish on the underside. This exquisite butterfly is becoming
Lycaena dispar increasingly rare, for it needs for its development exceptionally humid
Haworth ssp. *rutila* forests, bogs and similar water-logged localities, which are now becoming
Werneb. scarcer due to changes in land use. It has remained only in southeast
Europe, and even there it is quite rare.

Wsp ± 35 mm
Fpl Snake Root

Brown Hairstreak (180 — male, 181 and 182 — female) is the largest European Hairstreak, and
Thecla betulae L. if we take into account its Chinese subspecies, it is also one of the
largest Palaearctic Hairstreaks. It inhabits central Europe and extends
Wsp ± 40 mm from England as far east as Korea. This butterfly is fond of the margins
Fpl Blackthorn, Hawthorn,
Plum, Birch, Hazel, Poplar

of deciduous forests, of bushy slopes and rocks with hawthorn bushes, and occasionally it occurs even in natural parks and at the edges of large towns. It is coloured dark brown on the upper side, and at the tips of the hind wings there are small orange marks. The female has a large orange patch on the upper side of its forewings (182), whereas the male's wings only bear a faint hint of it. This makes the identification of the sexes very easy. The differences in the underside of their wings are not so striking. The white line on the hind wing of the female terminates roughly in the centre of the wing area (181), but on the male it continues, though less pronounced, to the other half of the wing (180).

The exotic Hairstreaks are magnificent. The butterflies of the genus *Ilerda* from the Himalayas and neighbouring region, have the undersides of their hind wings a vivid yellow with red decoration; the genus

Aphnaeus from the same area have a silvery zebra striping on their underwings; the species *Curebis acuta* from China has its wing underside pure white. Hairstreaks from the Indo-Australian, Etiopian and Neotropical areas are a dazzling sight with the metallic lustre of their azure-blue, yellow, green and ruby-red wings which, on the underside, are striped like a tiger's, or dotted like a jaguar's skin; others have spurs or trappings which are longer than the whole of their body. The refined mosaic pattern of the tropical Hairstreaks is in every conceivable colour, including silver and gold.

The larvae of the Blues do not resemble much other butterfly caterpillars. If they were not covered by hairs, they could be taken for smaller snails. The small head stays hidden under the rather flat body and is pushed out only if the caterpillar is feeding or moving from place to place when no danger threatens. If the larva of the Brown Hairstreak (183) is resting on the underside of a leaf, it is very inconspicuous. It hatches in the spring from the hibernated egg and from May till June feeds on hawthorn or blackthorn bushes.

183

184

Central Europe was the home to many species of Coppers, but today they are only very rarely to be come across there as many of them have become extinct.

Small Copper (184) was once the most abundant of all, with a tremendous range of distribution:
Lycaena phlaeas L. Europe and Asia, including the Arctic regions, parts of Africa and North
Wsp ± 25 mm America. Today this steppe-dweller survives only in localities where the
Fpl *Rumex acetosella* cultivated land has not pushed out completely the original wild nature.

Chalk-hill Blue (185) inhabits central Europe and penetrates eastwards as far as Iran. The male
Lysandra coridon Poda. is silvery blue on the upper side, with a dark brown outer border of the
wings. The female is dark brown. Both the sexes have their wing under-
Wsp ± 32 mm
Fpl *Coronilla*, Milk Vetch,
Horseshoe Vetch, Vetch
sides brown-green with black, white-rimmed spots. This butterfly is fond
of steppe regions, dry field borders and slopes, sandy hills overgrown
with wild vegetation, field tracks and paths, especially with lime-rich
substrate.

Harvester (186 left) was, until recently, classified in the family Lycaenidae in the Gerynini tribe.
Feniseca tarquinius Fab. In the modern work of W. H. Lowe it is ranked in the Liphyridae family.
It is the only American species whose caterpillars are predatory similarly
Wsp ± 32 mm
Fpl Aphids which live as
parasites on Alder, *Hamamelis*,
Hawthorn, Beech, Ash
to those of the Indo-Australian species. The upper side of its wings has
dark brown-grey underground decorated with dark dots inside large,
longitudinal, ochre-yellow areas. This butterfly is distributed mainly
in Atlantic coastal regions of North America as far as Florida and locally
to the west along the Gulf of Mexico and to the north to the central USA.

Great Blue Hairstreak (186 right), one of the larger species of the Theclini group, is the only
Atlides halesus Cr. American species with highly lustrous wings. Its homeland extends from
the southern part of the Atlantic coast (New Jersey) to Florida, to the
Wsp ± 37 mm west across Illinois to California and to the south across Mexico up to
Fpl *Quercus virginiana,* Costa Rica. The larger part of its wings is a glossy blue-green, of a similar
Phoradendron lustre as can be seen in the South American genus *Morpho*. The male's
forewings bear a brownish spot on black background.

Reakirt's Blue (186 below), one of the smallest American Blues, is coloured violet-blue from
Hemiargus izola above; the females are more or less brownish with bluish gloss at the
Reakirt wing roots. Hind wing tips show a relatively large dark eyespot and
several smaller ones. This species lives near the Great Lakes, on the
Wsp ± 18 mm coast of the Gulf of Mexico, in Mexico and Texas up to Costa Rica.
Fpl *Prosotis* (Viciales), Infrequently, it flies from the western Pacific coast as far as Canada.
Melilotis, Acacia, Indigofera

186

Chequered Blue occurs dispersively in some countries of central and southern Europe and to
Scolitantides orion Pall the east as far as Japan, being scarce in all its habitats. The upper side of
the wings is a dim brown with a blue tint. The outer margins are decorated
Wsp ± 30 mm
Fpl *Sedum telephium, S. album* with a band of pale grey-blue arches. The underside is grey-white with
and other species of *Sedum* black dots and an orange band along the outer borders of the hind wings.
The life of this species is dependent on the existence of stonecrop in the
lowlands and highlands. The strangely shaped caterpillars (187) lie
usually hidden under the lower leaves of stonecrops. Sometimes they
also live in ant-hills located in the vicinity of their foodplants.

Scarce Copper (188 — male) occurs in most parts of Europe and Asia as far as Mongolia.
Heodes virgaureae L.

Wsp ± 32 mm
Fpl Docks

188

189

159

Blue (189 — larva) is an inconspicuous, dark blue, small butterfly. It occurs sporadically in south-
Philotes vicrama   eastern Europe, in the south of central Asia up to northeastern India. The
schiffermülleri   caterpillars (189) live on flowering thyme.
Hemming

Wsp ± 20 mm
Fpl Thyme

The super-family of Skippers (Hesperioidea) is among the most numerous of diurnal butterflies. Its members are small to medium-sized, have a strong, conical body, wide head and robust thorax with short but powerful, firmly veined wings. They fly mostly during the daytime with the exception of some tropical species which fly at dusk and by night. About 3,000 species of this super-family are distributed over all inhabited continents, most of them being at home in South America. Tropical species are wonderfully coloured.

Arctic Skipper (190 left) is a small North American Skipper which inhabits central and southern
Carterocephalus   Canada, the north of the USA round the Great Lakes, almost all of
palemon Pallas   central Europe and partly also northern Europe, extending as far east
as the cooler regions of Asia. It is coloured dark brown with red-brown
Wsp ± 27 mm   spots.
Fpl Bromus, Grasses, *Poa*,
Calamagrostis

Checkered Skipper (190 right) is a thermophilous species of North America. Several of its varieties
Pyrgus communis Grote   occur locally from northern Canada to the south as far as Mexico, the
Antilles and Nicaragua. Eurasian representatives of the genus *Pyrgus*
Wsp ± 27 mm   inhabit mostly southern Europe and warmer parts of Asia. The wings of
Fpl Mallow, *Hibiscus, Abutilon*   this grey-brown butterfly are chequered in creamy white.

160

Chapter 8   THE GNOMES OF THE TROPICS

Nemeobiidae

There is yet another group of butterflies whose beauty not only equals that of the Blues, but sometimes even surpasses it. There are the very small butterflies of the family Nemeobiidae, which are closely related to the Lycaenids. Their caterpillars are thickly covered with short hairs, the pupae are suspended head downwards. This family consists of about 1,000 species which are scattered over the whole world. South and Central America, however, is the true home of most of them, with many of the most beautiful species.

Lyropteryx apollonia Westw. (191 — male) from Ecuador, Brazil and Bolivia, is velvety black with blue-green sheen and blood-red dots at the base of the wings. The underside of the wings is even more beautiful and most unusually coloured (192).

Wsp ± 40 mm

Duke of Burgundy Fritillary (193) is the only European representative of this family. It occurs dispersively in the temperate zones of Europe and in the east as far as central Asia.

Hamearis lucina L.

Wsp ± 28 mm
Fpl Primrose, Dock

191

192

193

Ancyluris aulestes Cr. ssp. **lamprotaenia** Stich (194, above — male's upper side) from Brazil
Wsp ± 32 mm   is one of the loveliest South American representatives.

Ancyluris formosissima Hew. (194, below — the underside) lives in Peru and Bolivia; in
Wsp ± 40 mm   the mountains it ascends to an altitude of up to 3,000 m.

Chapter 9

HAWK-MOTHS *Sphingidae*

Most of the members of the Hawk-moth family — Sphingidae — fly solely after dusk, and rest during the day. They are strong moths of medium and larger sizes, with robust bodies and powerful thoracic muscles. The body is covered with a thick layer of hairy scales in such a manner, that the head merges with the thorax and the conical abdomen. The whole body is perfectly stream-lined and therefore ideal for a swift, strong flight. The pair of powerful forewings, which are narrow, elongated and pointed at the end, serve together with the thoracic muscles as a propelling motor. Narrow wings and a short body give an aerodynamic combination which enables the Hawk-moths to be extremely versatile in their flight patterns. They are able to fly fast and straight and yet execute rapid turns or stops. A number of species are also able to hover.

Pine Hawk-moth (196) inhabits the coniferous forests of the Euro-Siberian region. During the *Hyloicus pinastri* L. day it rests on the bark of firs or pines (197), where its matching grey-brown colour provides an excellent protection. The greenish caterpillar

Wsp ± 75 mm
Fpl Pine, Silver Fir, Larch

(195), with yellow stripes and a reddish back is well hidden by the pine needles.

The wingspan of some of the South American Hawk-moths is as much as 25 cm.

195 196 197

Coequosa triangularis Don. (198) from the Indo-Australian region, measures up to 185 mm. The caterpillar is over 10 cm long, greenish in colour and covered with sharp spikes.

Wsp ± 150 mm
Fpl *Acacia, Banksia, Persoonia*

Privet Hawk-moth (199) is a Euro-Siberian species. Its caterpillar (200) resembles a sphinx.
Sphinx ligustri L.
Up to recently, caterpillars appeared rather commonly in city parks on privet and lilac shrubs. They pupate in the ground.

Wsp ± 100 mm
Fpl Privet, Lilac, Snowberry

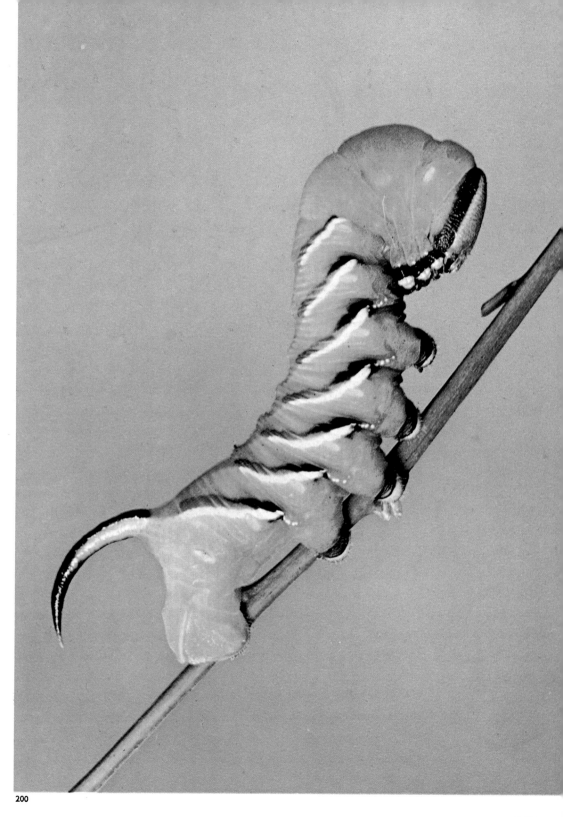

Convolvulus Hawk-moth (201, 205). This attractive and powerful moth migrates in some years
Herse convolvuli L. from the tropics of the Old World and from the Mediterranean regions
to the north. Across deserts, seas and Alpine mountain ranges leads the
Wsp ± 105 mm difficult journey of these fliers to the inhospitable north, sometimes as
Fpl *Convolvulus, Calystegia,* far as Iceland, right up to the Arctic Circle. During the warm nights of
Morning Glory, *Zygophyllum,* spring these champions race over a distance of thousands of kilometres,
Phaseolus flying either swiftly at higher altitudes, or lower down, resting occasionally on flowers. During the day they can be seen resting on poles, planks
and fences. They are almost invisible pressed against the wood, their
head up and the wings folded. The marvellous motor of muscles hidden

201

168

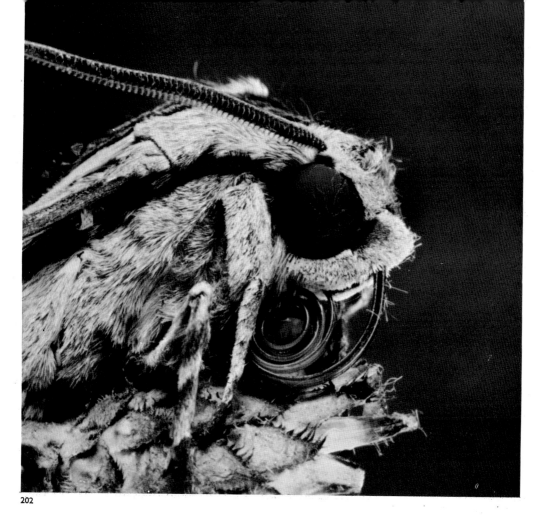

202

in the thorax — in volume almost one cubic centimetre — can conquer in just a few nights distances of thousands of kilometres, equalling as much as a quarter of the circumference of the Earth. This is one of the phenomena of nature at which mankind will never stop to marvel. The proboscis of Hawk-moths, especially of the Convolvulus Hawk-moth, is quite remarkable (202). Only some species which live permanently in the tropics have a longer proboscis. When the moth is not feeding the proboscis is coiled into a spiral and is not outwardly visible, being hidden from the sides by two hairy flaps. The photograph shows the proboscis before it is concealed. If the proboscis is carefully unwound, it will measure $\pm$ 90 mm, which is almost double the length of the moth's body! This of course enables the Convolvulus Hawk-moth to suck nectar from tubular flowers such as daturas as well as other tropical night-flowering plants. In the later evening it can be seen in

203

204

205

Europe on daturas, clematises, petunias, night primroses, soap-worts and tobacco plants. It is a marvellous experience to observe this quietly-humming moth, its mysterious, pink-grey body 'standing' in the air above flowers. With amazing coordination it probes each individual flower with the sensitive thread-like end of the proboscis, exerting its acrobatic skill to stop in the air at exactly the right spot. The green or blackish-brown caterpillar of Convolvulus Hawk-moth (203) is, together with the caterpillar of the Death's-head Hawk-moth, considered to be the largest European caterpillar. It feeds at night and during the day hides on the ground or a few centimetres underground. In central Europe it lives from July till August, hatching from eggs which were laid during the spring migration in May and June. The second immigration from the south occurs usually between the middle of August and middle of October. At one time the larvae could be easily found on dry, sunny slopes where convolvulus grew. Since the destruction of such biotypes it now occurs only rarely in potato fields where convolvulus weeds are present. The pupa of the Convolvulus Hawk-moth (204) is easily recognized by the unusual way in which the proboscis case is curved.

Oleander Hawk-moth (206, 207, 208, 210) flies from the south to central and northern Europe
Daphnis nerii L.   similarly to the Convolvulus Hawk-moth. It is, however, a much rarer
visitor. The beauty of the green and mauve-pink shades of its colour

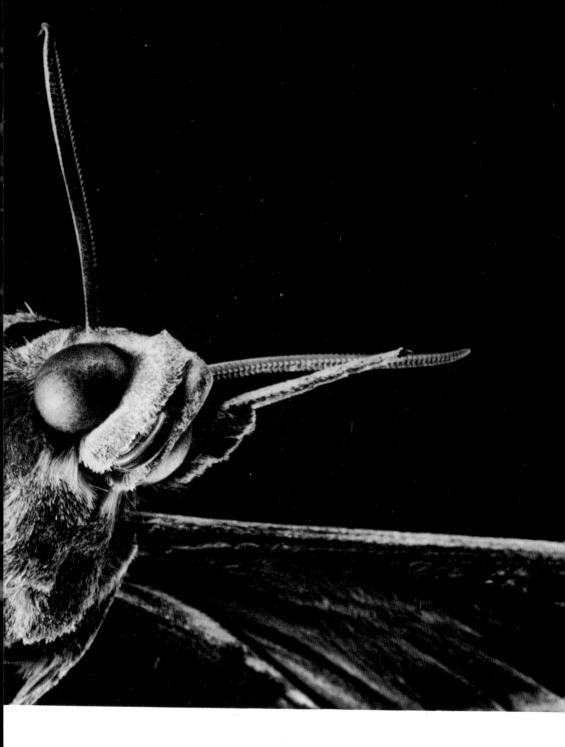

Wsp ± 100 mm
Fpl *Nerium oleander*
(*Vinca, Asclepias*)

and the elegance of shape places the Oleander Hawk-moth among the loveliest of moths and butterflies on Earth. In southern Europe this species develops regularly two or even more generations, and it can be seen during daytime resting on bushes or tree trunks. The imago hatches from the chrysalis usually about midnight; during the rest of the night the wings develop and grow firm and after a day's rest in the warm sun, the moth is ready for its first night flight. It awakens from the day's sleep when the sun goes down, and flies to feed on nectar-containing nocturnal flowers. When fed and refreshed it flies into the night to seek

207

208

a partner for pairing. After mating which takes place during the hottest nights, it migrates to remote countries. There the females lay the green round eggs on the oleanders, planted in flower pots in front of houses and in gardens; often several eggs are placed on one bush. This happens because in central and northern Europe oleander does not grow wild,

175

being bound to more Mediterranean climate. In the tropics the caterpillar develops also on several other plants, upon which the female
Hawk-moth lays its eggs.

Apart from the Mediterranean region, the Oleander Hawk-moth inhabits the whole of Africa up to its most southern tip, Madagascar, subtropical and tropical Asia, including south India and Sri Lanka. In these
warm regions it is much more abundant than in the north, where it is
only rarely found. The pupa of the Oleander Hawk-moth is also beautiful
(209). It is light brown with respiratory holes rimmed in black; it also
has a straight black line on the underside of the head and thorax, and is
approximately 5 cm long. We can find it on the ground among the fallen
leaves or in the ground not far from oleander bushes. It is usually in
a very loose cocoon, often only in several threads which join up dry
leaves. For any collector of butterflies it is an uncommon event when
someone brings pupae or caterpillars of this magnificent Hawk-moth
from southern Europe. Mainly the southern half of the east coast of the
Adriatic Sea, with regions round Dubrovnik, Zagreb and Rijeka provide
the most fruitful localities for collectors. Ragged leaves of oleander and

210

even more, dark droppings under the bush, which resemble grains of pepper, are the tell-tale marks of the caterpillar's presence. If the oleander bushes are empty, without any sign of the caterpillars, this can only mean they have already pupated and so it is necessary to search through the fallen leaves and twigs under the bush. If we are lucky and have a suitable box, the pupae can be carefully transferred. At home they must be placed in a roomy cage with rough, upright walls, preferably from wire netting, so that the moths, once they emerge, can climb up the walls and suspend themselves on the ceiling, to enable the wings to develop and harden. Until the emerging of the imago the pupae of the Oleander Hawk-moth must be kept in a dry and warm place. This rule, however, does not apply generally for other Hawk-moth species. If we are in luck and find caterpillars of the Oleander Hawk-moth on an oleander bush (211, 212), it is also fairly safe to transfer them in a box. Of course they need sufficient food for the journey — and this applies to all caterpillars. Insufficient light in the box is immaterial, for many caterpillars feed only at night and seek their food by their sense of smell. Caterpillar's eyes are not very discernible, and form groups of simple larvae eyes (stemata) at the side of the head. These compound eyes are placed one at each side in the front, near the proboscis. Both halves of the head, which seem to be the caterpillar's eyes, are only chitinous covers for the powerful muscles, which govern the movement of the mandibles. If we watch closely the perfect work of this biting apparatus, with its glands and other

211

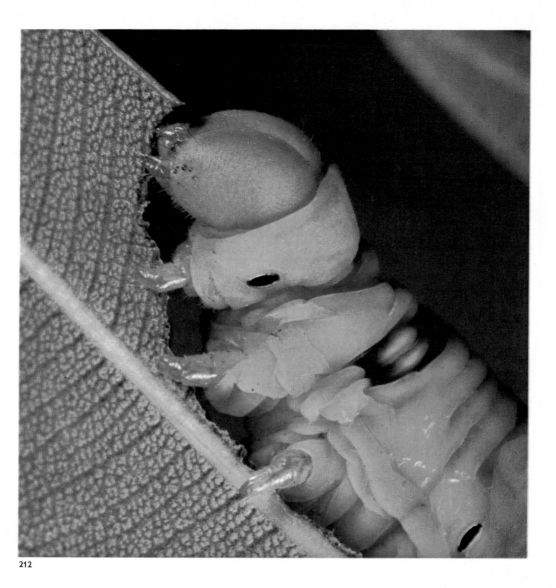

212

additional organs, we marvel how quickly a leaf disappears. To ensure the development of a perfect and healthy butterfly, the caterpillar must have a constant and sufficient food supply and must not go hungry even for a short time.

Many butterflies and moths captured in the wild are damaged, and it is the natural desire of any collector to own perfect specimens with uninjured wings. From a correctly fed larva (in collections this is classified as 'ex larvae') it is possible to rear a faultless specimen. It follows therefore that the best way to augment a collection is by catching caterpillars and rearing them in captivity. When collecting caterpillars of unknown species, it is also vital to note which foodplant they are feeding on, to ensure the correct feeding in captivity. It is a great asset, therefore, if the collector or breeder is well versed in botany.

213

Death's head Hawk-moth (213—221) with its skull-like design on its thorax is one of the most
Acherontia atropos L. interesting sights among European moths. This unusual design in-
fluenced its scientific name. Linné, in 1758, introduced its specific name
after the feared Greek goddess, who, in any fateful moment, has the
Wsp ± 110 mm right to decide between life and death . . . In 1809 the scientist Laspeyres
Fpl Solanaceae, Daucaceae, gave it the generic name after a river in the mythical Hades. The genus
Cherry Plum, Willow, *Acherontia* is poor in species. Apart from *A. atropos* there are two other
Mulberry, Lilac, Ash, Walnut, species inhabiting the Old World: *A. lachesis* F. and *A. styx* Ww., both
Privet, Apple, Pear, *Rubia,* from the Indo-Malayan region. (Lachesis was one of the goddesses, who
Verbascum, Viciales, could cut the thin thread of life, Styx was a river in Hades). Both
Zygophyllum, Urticaceae, these species are fairly alike the European one, and have similar design
Philadelphus, Strawberry, on their thorax.
Cornus, Honeysuckle,
Erigeron, Oleaceae,
Chenopodiaceae, Vine

180

214

It is every breeder's dream to witness the unforgettable moment of a young Death's-head Hawk-moth emerging from the pupa with its wings still tiny and soft (213, 214).

At first the young imago nervously climbs the sides of the rearing cage, till it finds a suitable spot for suspending itself so that the slowly growing wings would have ample space for development. During their 'growth', when the still soft tissues fill with air and blood and gradually harden, the two upper surfaces of the wings remain pressed against each other. The well-known design on the back is greatly distorted when the wings are in such a position, so that hardly anything is visible of the famous pattern of this moth (215). Not until approximately two hours later, when the wings and the body harden completely, does the moth

181

flap over its wings in a roof-like position (216). Now the Death's-head Hawk-moth can be seen in all its splendour. A human face stares at us from the back side of the thorax. Two eyes, something resembling a moustache, an oval crown of the head, scattered design which could be taken for a mouth or chin . . . However, the ancient human fantasy sought evil signs and warnings of death everywhere and so the design received a mysterious and terrifying meaning — it was regarded as the image of a human skull. And the pale yellow lines under the face were taken to be the crossed bones . . . (217). Throughout the whole area of this moth's occurrence, people used to take this chance arrangement of dots and lines for an evil sign.

The strange design on the thorax of the Death's-head Hawk-moth is created by variably coloured scales, which are similar to those which cover the whole body of the moth. Hawk-moths have some of the scales elongated to form a sort of hair.

216

217

The proboscis of the Death's-head Hawk-moth is very interesting (218). The illustration shows a newly emerged moth before the wings become separated and before the proboscis is properly coiled and hidden. Though it measures only about 1 cm, it is strong, hard and firm. Both halves have a sharp tip at the end. The proboscis serves to suck from shallow flowers and from injured trees and is well equipped to pierce the wax lids of the honey cells in a honey-comb. The Death's-head also uses its proboscis most effectively in self-defence, when piercing someone's finger. In the temperate zone of the Mediterranean, Death's-heads have been found inside bee-hives, which they entered in search of honey.

218

Even in northern countries to which they had flown from the south, they were on rare occasions found inside hives. The small intake of honey is harmless, but the moths disturb the bees.

The female migrating from the south to central Europe lays her eggs mostly individually on potato plants, but also on leaves of plants of the nightshade family. Following its activity during the night, we can find the Death's-head resting near the plant where its eggs were laid, or sitting on a fence or a wall (219, 220). The male can be recognized by its short, slender and pointed abdomen. The female is much bigger and has a wider, longer and bluntly tipped abdomen (221).

221

The Death's-head Hawk-moth is rarely injured in its natural habitat. Its surface is protected by the soft, but firmly attached covering of hairy scales. All the same, the most beautiful specimens can only be obtained when rearing them from pupae in captivity (222, 224).

For collectors of butterflies and moths it is a rare feat to find the Death's-head's caterpillar (223). Usually it is discovered purely by chance, though there are experts who manage to find one every year. This calls for much experience and time, perseverence and tirelessness and a certain amount of dedication. In central Europe, the caterpillar was once most frequently found in potato fields. The bitten tops of the potato plants and the fresh droppings on the ground give away the spot where the caterpillar had feasted in the night. During the day it hides in the dense greenery on the ground, or crawls just a centimetre or two underground. When disturbed, it raises the forequarters of its body and if irritated, it wags its head. Some emit strange squealing sounds by means of mandibles. This is one of the largest caterpillars found in

222

Europe; it is said it can be up to 15 cm long. The size of the caterpillar depends on the number of warm nights during which it feeds. The time of its growth and its lifespan also depends on temperature. In the southern warm regions the caterpillar sometimes lives only two weeks, whereas in the north it can survive for more than two months! When breeding in captivity, we can shorten the caterpillar stage by raising the temperature and the food intake; the larvae will get accustomed to feed even in daytime. It is advisable to feed the caterpillar with its natural foodplant even in captivity, even if it is polyphagous and can live on various other plants (this larva, for instance, on fifty different species). The colouring is not distinct: it can be shades of yellow, green, brown, or ochre-brown. When fully grown, the larva wanders for a long time. Rearing the caterpillars at home it is necessary therefore to create the right conditions for this activity. The pupae reared in captivity are always a better guarantee of a healthy moth than pupae found by chance during the harvesting of potatoes, which are usually collected by laymen. The

189

223

mature caterpillar first wets its body with saliva, then ourrows ínto the ground. At a depth of 15—30 cm it smooths out an egg-shaped chamber to pupate in. Then it coats the inner surface of the chamber with saliva, which cements the soil particles together. After some time, several days in fact, it changes into a pupa. In illustration 222 we can see by the rear end of the body the discarded skin of the caterpillar — exuvium. If we were unable to find the caterpillar, it would be much harder to look for its pupa. The caterpillar, before pupating, often travels and crawls into the ground far from the plant on which it left feeding traces. The pupae are most frequently found during the potato harvest. When using mechanization, many are broken, but a few remain undamaged. To have an unharmed pupa is the first concern. To look after it in captivity in the right manner, is the second concern. Lepidopterists have many years

224

of experience with each species of these insects. The pupae of the Oleander Hawk-moth need warm and dry conditions, whereas the pupae of the Death's-head require dampness and warmth. I had read and heard many instructions on how to breed the Death's-head Hawk-moth — for instance to place the pupae into special tubes, etc. But I preferred to work with damp earth, peat, moss, wet rags and polyvinyl-chloride. In the terrarium placed on a sunny balcony, the young Death's-head always emerged. In normal, warm weather the Hawk-moths of the second generation in central Europe will hatch in the middle or during the second half of September. The females which emerge from these pupae are considered to be barren, but it is said that after the return to the south they are capable of further breeding. Though the two sexes of the Death's-head can mate in captivity, no one as yet has been able to induce the females to lay eggs. If the sitting Death's-head is irritated, it gives out a squeaking sound and flutters its wings fiercely. This exhibits the vivid yellow stripes on the hind wings and the black-and-yellow striped abdomen.

Striped Hawk-moth (225) is distributed through the Old World tropical and subtropical regions.
Celerio livornica Esp. The colours of this lovely moth are olive-brown, white, black, light ochre, while the central flames on the hind wings are a vivid pink. It has two marginal light bands on its thorax. On very rare occasions individual moths reach central Europe from Africa, and the females lay eggs, from which caterpillars hatch. These are usually blue-green, yellow

Wsp ± 80 mm
Fpl Vine, Willowherb,
Bedstraw, Dock, Spurge,
Toadflax, *Antirrhinum*, Thistle

225

226

at both ends. Their body generally has groups of yellow dots, but they can be coloured differently and have a completely different design. In the east this moth occurs as far as south India and China, and also inhabits Australia. In the Americas a related species, called the Striped Morning Sphinx (*C. lineata* Fab.) is found. It differs from *C. livornica* in the number of bands on the thorax.

Celerio vespertilio Esp. (226) has grey-brown forewings with a barely visible light slanting stripe and a centre spot. The hind wings are clear pink with black corners at the base and black band along the outer margins. The body is grey, the abdomen has black and light lateral stripes. This Hawk-moth inhabits some countries of southern and southeastern Europe; it occurs in the east in several countries round the Caucasus, for instance in Armenia. Warm, dry regions are its favourite habitat, and there its caterpillar lives generally on plants which grow on rocks.

Wsp ± 65 mm
Fpl Bedstraw, Willowherb, Lythrum

193

Bedstraw Hawk-moth
Celerio galii Rott.

Wsp ± 65 mm
Fpl Bedstraw, Willowherb,
Asperula, Spurge, *Fuchsia,*
Willow

(227) is one of the most beautiful Hawk-moths of Europe. Its coloration is very gay consisting of at least five colours. A Holarctic steppe species, it occurs in the Palaearctic region and also in North America. The American form *C. g. intermedia* Ky. inhabits the area stretching from Canada to Colorado and Georgia. In Eurasia this particular Hawk-moth is spread from the western shores of Europe right up to Japan. The occurrence of this species, as far as population is concerned, has in the past varied considerably from year to year. In some years these moths were relatively common and occurred in two generations; in other years they were scarce. In 1949 they were still most numerous in Thuringia in Germany. In 1950 there was such an overpopulation of this species round Nurem-

A Hawk-moth sucking from plants in flight

berg that the masses of caterpillars, which were said to total more than 100,000, devoured all foodplants acceptable to them (mainly yellow bedstraw and willowherbs). The larvae which did not manage to pupate before all food disappeared, died of hunger. The overpopulation of the American form of this moth was also known in the past.

Celerio galii is a vagrant; it is fond of undertaking long flights. Though it is the species which penetrates far into the north and prefers to live at higher elevations, it is still considered to be a steppe species, for its larvae are found on yellow bedstraw plants and various rock willows. The first generation generally hatches at the end of May and the beginning of June. The second generation appears in August and September, when conditions are favourable (warm, dry summers). With the advancement of agricultural mechanization, this species has now been practically wiped out from many countries of central Europe. It suffered the same fate as the Spurge Hawk-moth, which is now also almost extinct in these countries, though not so long ago it was the most common Hawk-moth. The caterpillar of *Celerio galii* (228) is either green with yellow dots, or black-brown with yellow dots. As in all true Hawk-moths, it has curved horn at the end of its body.

228

229

Spurge Hawk-moth (229–233, 242, 244) was originally distributed through all the Palaearctic
Celerio euphorbiae L. region including southern Europe and North Africa as far as southwestern
India and north China. Another migrating moth-vagrant, it was, until
recently, one of the most abundant Hawk-moths of central Europe. Its
Wsp ± 70 mm
Fpl *Euphorbia cyparissias* beautiful caterpillars (233) were, about fifty years ago, an everyday sight

196

230

231

232

198

233

on field-boundaries, sandy fallow land and dry grassy pastures, where cypress spurge grew. It is surprising that this migrant moth is no longer seen even in localities, which have not been destroyed and where this plant still grows. It appears that this beautiful Hawk-moth was particularly susceptible to air-pollution and to chemicals applied in agricultural development, which affected even the remaining original steppe localities.

234

Protambulyx eurycles H.S. (234) is a tropical Hawk-moth of outstanding beauty and elegance of shape. The elongated, powerful wings range it among the most perfect fliers. The tropical range of South America is its habitat. Its colouring is olive-brown and a vivid ochre yellow. The green yellow-spotted caterpillar has an almost straight long horn and orange dots at the sides of its body.

Wsp ± 115 mm
Fpl Anacardiaceae

235

Small Elephant Hawk-moth (235, 236, 237) is the smallest of the Hawk-moths of central Europe.
Deilephila porcellus L. The relatively short wings, chubby body and pink colouring influenced its rather apt Latin name — *porcellus* (piglet). This is a Euro-Siberian steppe moth, whose area of distribution covers central and other more temperate parts of Europe in the east stretching as far as Transcaucasia. In recent years *Deilephila porcellus* has become a rarity, though this fact

Wsp ± 45 mm
Fpl *Galium verum* (other species of *Galium*, Willow-herb, *Lythrum*, Vine)

201

236

is not always admitted in literature, where it is still quoted to be 'abundant in places', 'fairly abundant', 'widespread', etc. This applied to the past, when sandy hillsides, knolls and slopes were still covered with the original steppe flowers. The Small Elephant Hawk-moth, a beautiful ornament of nature in central Europe, is a typical example of how the face of nature in central Europe has changed. Fifty years ago they were frequently seen at the onset of the warm nights as it was growing dark, at the end of May and beginning of June.

The caterpillar of *Deilephila porcellus* (238) can be found during the night on field-boundaries overgrown with yellow bedstraw (*Galium verum*). During daytime it hides under the plants and only in darkness crawls to the surface. Usually it is dark grey in colour, sometimes

237

238

green. The characteristic horn at the rear end of the young caterpillar disappears with its development. The caterpillar pupates in a loose
cocoon on mossy ground under the plant, where it usually also hibernates.
Only very exceptionally it hatches in autumn of the same year, thus
forming the second generation, which of course dies out with the arrival
of winter.

239

Elephant Hawk-moth (239, 241) resembles the preceding species, but is substantially bigger.
Deilephila elpenor L. The pink colouring is interlaced in places with olive-green stripes. This also is a Euro-Siberian steppe species which inhabits almost the entire warmer and temperate Palaearctic region, occurring in several different aberrations. On rare occasions it can be seen after dark hovering above garden flowers or flowering yellow irises by ponds.

Wsp ± 63 mm
Fpl Willowherb, *Lythrum,* Balsam, Bedstraw, *Balsamina,* Vine, *Rubia,* Honeysuckle, *Fuchsia, Ampelopsis*

The caterpillars of the Elephant Hawk-moth (240) are relatively big

and conspicuous. They occur in two different colorations; most frequently they are dark. Similarly to the caterpillar of the preceding species, they have behind their head two pairs of fairly large dark spots, which on irritation stand out like big black eyes. The caterpillar raises the forequarters of its body, draws the front segments together in such a manner that it appears as if a widened 'head' has formed, which, together with the lateral spots, resembles a fearsome object, very like a snake's head. Compared with the caterpillars of *Deilephila porcellus*, these larvae have

241

only a short horn. In central Europe, the caterpillars of the Elephant Hawk-moth pupate at the end of August into a yellow-brown, black-dotted chrysalis, hidden in the remnants of plants and under the moss. From the pupae of the first fertile generation the moth hatches in spring of the following year, but some hibernate yet another winter. The moths of the first brood appear in May and June. Unfortunately it seems that even this Hawk-moth has almost disappeared, though its foodplants have not on the whole been destroyed.

Pergesa (Theretra) alecto L. (243) has a reddish-brown colouring, with the centres of the hind
wings vividly pink-red. It inhabits the area stretching from the Mediter-
ranean islands to the east as far as Indo-Malayan tropics.

Wsp ± 75 mm
Fpl Vine, *Psychotria*

Upon irritation, the Spurge Hawk-moth reacts characteristically by
flipping its body up and down (244). Its yellow-brown pupae (242) some-

245

times hatch after only 16 days, sometimes not till five years later. The reason for this has not yet been explained.

Celerio hybr. **harmuthi** Kordesch (245) is a crossbreed of the Spurge Hawk-moth male and the Elephant Hawk-moth female. To achieve this, the expert must feed tens and hundreds of caterpillars, reared from eggs, and then tend them till the moths hatch. It takes much patience based on great experience before artificial copulation between different species and sometimes even different genera can be achieved. Success in this field came to the Prague entomologist, Jan Pokorný, in 1961, when it was still possible to find the larvae of both these species. Perhaps this may have been the last opportunity to attempt such an experiment, for in the following years both the species of Hawk-moths became extinct.

Wsp The illustrated male measured 50 mm

Poplar Hawk-moth (246, 248) shows the colours of its hind wings only at the moment of arriving
Laothoë populi L. and settling on the bark of a tree, before folding them into a resting
position. This is a typical member of a special group of Hawk-moths,

Wsp ± 75 mm
Fpl Poplar, Willow, Ash, Birch

which at one time were classified by Lathreille by the generic name of
Smerinthus. They differ from the true Hawk-moths by the larger, broader,
notched wings, the short proboscis which is unable to take food and by
other less distinct anatomical features. The Poplar Hawk-moth is a most
attractive and interesting moth, immensely variable in its colouring, so
that it is not possible to find two exactly alike specimens. It occurs in
various shades of grey and brown, often with a greenish tint. At other
times its wings display various hues of rusty red.

The Poplar Hawk-moth inhabits the Palaearctic region, where it is
extremely widespread. The area of distribution stretches from England

246

247

across Europe and Siberia to Altai. It is seen wherever the trees it feeds upon grow. In the mountains it lives relatively high, over 1,200 m. Similarly to all Hawk-moths, this species has become also increasingly rare in Europe. It can be encountered most often at the end of May, in June or July; sometimes, the moths of the second generation appear in August. During the daytime, we come across it most frequently on poplar and aspen trunks, where it climbed during the preceding night after hatching from the pupa. The pupa usually lays from the preceding summer just below the ground under the foodplants of the caterpillars. The pupa (247) is black-brown, thickset, with blunt ends and without the proboscis sheath. The ground round the trees in the lowland woods and river growths where the caterpillar lives is usually damp, and this is beneficial to the pupae. If the Poplar Hawk-moth is bred in captivity, it is necessary to keep the pupae in adequate damp conditions, to ensure the hatching of healthy, well-developed moths.

An earlier name, *Amorpha*, described the shape of this 'shapeless' moth very accurately, for when still (248), it is more akin to a young aspen leaf than to a live moth. When in this position, the Hawk-moth's under-wings jut out sideways, but the conspicuous rusty stains of the hind wings stay hidden under the upper wings. The dully coloured, dentated margins mark the outline of the sitting moth and make it merge with the young foliage. The antennae on the picture are purposely pushed outwards, so the photo would not lack in didactic value; normally they stay hidden at the sides under the front segments of the body.

The almost immobile caterpillar of the Poplar Hawk-moth (249) usually lives on the low undergrowth of trees it feeds upon. During the day it sits

249

motionless first on the underside of the leaf, later on the twig, with the head inclined to the ventral side. In central Europe it occurs in the period between June and beginning of October. Its colouring is usually green with yellow diagonal lines and red-brown lateral spots, but occasionally the basic colouring is yellowish or whitish. The horn is light-coloured; the lower diagonal yellow side-stripes meet here, which makes its sides light. The length of an adult female caterpillar can be up to 9 cm. The male larvae are usually smaller.

Eyed Hawk-moth (250, 252, 253, 255) is, without doubt, the most beautiful Hawk-moth of *Smerinthus ocellatus* L. Europe. The scarlet-brown upper wings cover the underwings which can be seen only when the moth is disturbed. The red area of the hind

Wsp ± 75 mm
Fpl Willow, Poplar, Apple, Pear, Plum·

wings is ornamented with eyespots, emphasized by their black rim. Thin black centres are circled in blue, imitating the iris. The effect of the two strikingly coloured eyespots, which suddenly seem to focus upon a predator, is quite startling.

251

252

The blue-green caterpillar of the Eyed Hawk-moth (251, 254) is very similar to the caterpillar of the Poplar Hawk-moth. The basic colouring is fairly changeable, but the horn has dark sides.

The copulation of the Eyed Hawk-moth (253) usually starts during the warm summer evenings and the mating lasts through the following day till the evening. The female, which is the stronger of the two, holds on to a solid object and the male hangs upon the female, generally head pointing downwards, the legs pressed against the body.

254

Illustration 254 shows a young, 13 mm-long caterpillar of the Eyed Hawk-moth. The developing caterpillars of Hawk-moths are often gayer in colour than the adult larvae. The surface structure is usually also more striking, especially when several times magnified.

256

Oak Hawk-moth (256, 260, 261) is one of the loveliest Hawk-moths of the Old World, despite its rather simple colouring. It can be all possible shades of ochre, sometimes turning to brown, other times to reddish. The resemblance to a dry leaf is so strong, that it merges completely with the undergrowth of Turkey oak, where it is most likely to be found. There are several tens of species of the *Marumba* genus living in the more southern countries of Palaearctic Asia and in the tropic regions of Asia, but this is the only species which occurs in southern Europe, the north boundary of its range being southern Slovakia.

Marumba quercus Den. et Schiff.

Wsp ± 90 mm
Fpl *Quercus cerris* (and other species of Oak), Holly

257

The caterpillar of the Oak Hawk-moth (257, 258, 259) is blue-green with a granular surface, white oblique stripes at the sides of body, brownish respiratory holes and yellow-brown legs. The head is green, with lighter wart-like bulges. A vertical row of skin-coloured warts can be observed at each side of the head. This caterpillar moves very little, and if reared in captivity, it is necessary to make sure it crawls on to fresh food, or to transfer it there carefully. So as not to tear the prolegs off the leaf, it is recommended to cut carefully round the leaf as close to the resting caterpillar as possible and then lay the larva with the remnant of the leaf on the fresh food. It must be kept in an airy cage,

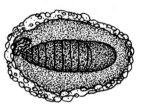

Pupa of the Oak
Hawk-moth in a firm
clayey cover

258

259

The rear end of pupa of the
Oak Hawk-moth viewed
from above

260

for it cannot bear the close atmosphere in a glass. The larvae of the Oak Hawk-moth are also very sensitive to disturbances during the moulting period, which sometimes lasts up to three days, and is repeated four times during the caterpillar's life. Now and again someone brings a fertilized female or a pair into central Europe from the Mediterranean. They mate fairly easily and soon afterwards the female lays the eggs. The Oak Hawk-moths are usually seen resting low on the undergrowth or on fairly thin trunks of oaks or cerium up to 8 cm in diameter. The moths, when at rest, are very similar to dry leaves (260, 261).

261

Lime Hawk-moth (262, 263, 264) is one of the species which still can be found in central Europe.
Mimas tiliae L. The polyphagous character of the caterpillar which feeds upon a large assortment of deciduous trees helps this most attractive moth to survive in spite of its many enemies — ichneumon flies, braconids, parasitic flies, pheasants, moles and bats — all consumers of moths. This particular Hawk-moth is changeable in colour and design, especially as far as the markings on the forewings are concerned. The central cross-band is sometimes broken; the colouring is often skin yellow-brown with olive-green spots and stripes; less frequently, the colouring is brownish to

Wsp ± 65 mm
Fpl Lime, Birch, Willow, Alder, Hornbeam, Elm, Oak, Cherry Plum, Walnut, Ash, Pear, Apple, Horse Chestnut

reddish. The specimens where the basic colour is pinkish and the spots are green are extremely beautiful. The underside of this moth is most commonly ochre with greenish stripes at the borders of the wings (262). It can be seen in such a position only when freshly hatched generally before noon during the warm days of May or June. A few hours later, when the wings are fully developed and hardened, the moth swings them to the sides (263), so that they resemble two young green leaves on a twig. It is interesting to note that this moth avoids enclosed forest growths even when they contain trees upon which its caterpillar feeds. If the tree avenues along roads were all felled, we would not only destroy the beauty of the countryside, but could also list this species among the extinct moths.

263

264

The Lime Hawk-moth belongs to the moths which seldom wander far from where their larvae lived and where they hatched. In contrast to some other Hawk-moths, their caterpillar lives high in the crowns of trees, and is therefore difficult to find. Most frequently it can be found under trees after violent storms or hailstorms etc., or if it has just left the treetops in order to pupate by the foot of the same tree. It is green with a granular surface, similar to the caterpillars of the two species described on the preceding pages. It differs in the coloration of the tail horn which is green or blue; the yellow oblique stripes at the sides of body are, on one side, rimmed in red. The caterpillar crawls just under the ground or buries itself among dry foliage, and pupates in a very loose cocoon. The pupa is dark grey-brown, with a wrinkled surface, immobile, and gives the impression of being dead and dried up. The moths hatch mostly the next spring, or on rare occasions towards autumn of the same year. Alternately it can happen that they do not hatch till two years later. This Hawk-moth is distributed throughout nearly all of the European Palaearctic region reaching as far east as Transcaucasia.

265

Willowherb Hawk-moth (265, 266, 267) is in coloration somewhat alike the Lime Hawk-moth,
Proserpinus
proserpina Pal.
but much smaller in size. It is equally attractive and has the elongated proboscis of the *Macroglossum* genera. These are Hawk-moths found in all opportune parts of the world. They are noted for small sizes, long antennae and flat widened body, framed at the end of the abdomen and at the sides by tufts of hair, often strikingly coloured. The tropical species especially manifest this feature. This equipment helps them to soar in the air. Some genera of these small Hawk-moths have semi-transparent or almost transparent wings with scaleless areas. The

Wsp ± 43 mm
Fpl Evening Primrose, Willowherb, (*Lythrum, Fuchsia*)

266

Willowherb Hawk-moth has non-transparent wings which are usually olive-green, sometimes pinkish. The hind wings are ochre yellow with a black border. The hind wings and especially the forewings are deeply indentated. This rare moth inhabits some localities of central and southern Europe, and to the east is found as far as the eastern parts of central Asia. It keeps to the original steppe or wooded steppe localities overgrown with willowherb, on which its caterpillars mostly feed. These are grey-brown, occasionally green with black lines, and have no horn. They pupate just beneath the ground, where the red-brown pupae hibernate. The moth hatches in May to June.

268

Hummingbird Hawk-moth (268) has brown-grey upper surface of the forewings with black
Macroglossum cross-lines and rusty brown hind wings, which darken at the base and by
stellatarum L. the borders. The widened, flat abdomen with gaily coloured hair tufts
is rather interesting; during flight it opens at the back like the birds'
Wsp ± 45 mm tail quills. The moths occur in Europe from June to October in two
Fpl Bedstraw, *(Stellaria, Rubia)* generations. Apart from this, moths from the south migrate into central
and northern Europe and Asia already in May. The Hummingbird
Hawk-moth is a migrating vagrant of the south, which travels over
great distances. The extensive favourable area of the Palaearctic region
is its habitat; in the east it occurs in the subtropical parts of western
Asia as far as tropical south India.

230

269

The caterpillar of the Hummingbird Hawk-moth (269) could still be found several decades ago on dry slopes, field boundaries and hillsides. It feeds even during the day, which is in contrast to most Hawk-moth caterpillars which stay hidden in daytime and feed only at night. The gnawed leaves of bedstraw show its presence. Its coat is green or brown-green, with white dots and stripes and with a short, sharp horn at the end of the body. It is 35 mm long and the head is laterally flattened. It pupates in the ground or under plants on the ground, changing into a light yellow-brown chrysalis with a dark thoracic stripe running between the bases of the future wings.

The moths of the Eggar family (Lasiocampidae) are distributed throughout favourable regions of the Earth in about 1,200 species. They are usually medium or large-sized, with relatively inconspicuous colouring and rounded, stout, shaggy bodies; their wings are rounded and short. Vividly coloured species, with elongated and narrow bodies occur only in the tropics, particularly in the Old World. The Eggars have a rudimentary proboscis and therefore cannot feed. The eyes are small, and the simple eyes are lacking. The antennae are shortly combed and the males are commonly much smaller than the females. Their hearing organ has not yet been identified. The larvae are always hairy, pupae are enveloped in relatively perfect cocoons. The eggs are usually laid gregariously.

270

271

Lappet (271, 273) is one of the largest Palaearctic species. It inhabits areas stretching from the
Gastropacha eastern shores of the Atlantic as far east as China and Japan. The copper-
quercifolia L. reddish wings have dentated edges and when at rest, the underwings
jut out slightly sideways from under the upper ones. In this position
Wsp ± 75 mm – female the moth matches perfectly a dead leaf. The moth emerges in Europe
Fpl Blackthorn, Rowan, during July and August from a membranous cocoon (270) of dark grey
Willow, Hazel, Apple, Pear, colour, which is usually inconspicuously attached to a branch. The
Plum inside of the pupa is egg-shaped, black-brown, and covered in whitish
powder. An empty cocoon is illustrated here; we can recognize it by the
pale liquid maconium, which trickles out when the moth is leaving
the cocoon.

233

272

The caterpillars of the Lappet (272) are flat underneath, so that they are well able to press against a branch of a tree or a bush. Their colouring is most variable. The illustration does not show the two blue cross-stripes

273

behind the head, which appear suddenly if the caterpillar is provoked. When resting on bark, it is almost impossible to find; it is perfectly camouflaged. The female caterpillars can measure up to 12 cm. They hatch from the eggs (279) in September, feed during the night and by winter grow up to a length of 2—3 cm. The caterpillars hibernate close to the branch or the bark of a tree, surviving hard frost, sleet and icy winds. The next spring they resume feeding, like most larvae of the Eggar family in these regions. In July they pupate, and the moths emerge after two weeks. Regular spraying of fruit trees has almost wiped out this moth from gardens.

Pine Lappet (274) is distributed in parts of the Euro-Siberian region. The grey-brown colouring
Dendrolimus pini L.   of this moth is uncommonly variable, mimicking the bark of the pine.
It lives from June to August and in years of overpopulation it used to
Wsp ± 60 mm
Fpl Pine, Fir   cause damage in forests. The caterpillar hibernates on the forest ground.

Cocoon with pupa of the
Oak Eggar

276

Oak Eggar (275 — female) occurs in the Euro-Siberian area, mostly in mixed or oak woods of higher elevations, particularly near peat-bogs. The female, which is much bigger than the male, is light ochre and the male is dark red-brown with an ochre band across the wings. The caterpillar hibernates and the pupa has a striking barrel-shaped, firm cocoon.

Lasiocampa quercus L.

Wsp ± 65 mm
Fpl Bilberry, Blackberry, Oak, Willow, Birch

Small Eggar (276) is another Euro-Siberian species, favouring wooded steppes with lime ground. Its colouring is dark red-brown. The black-brown caterpillars (277) are decorated with two rows of red spots and live gregariously in large nests.

Eriogaster lanestris L.

Wsp ± 33 mm
Fpl Cherry, Plum, Birch, Hawthorn, Willow, Lime

277

The barrel-shaped chrysalides sometimes hibernate several times. The eggs form ring clusters round a twig, covered with hair. They cause a small amount of damage.

Grass Eggar (278) resembles slightly the Oak Eggar in design, but its coloration is red-brown, sometimes turning to grey. The Grass Eggar is distributed from the temperate and southern Europe eastwards to Transcaucasia. A steppe species, it lives in dry original localities. The moth emerges from June to September, the caterpillar lives from May to June. Then it spins a firm, barrel-shaped, dark grey cocoon. In the temperate zone, this moth hibernates in the egg-stage; it is often destroyed in this stage by fire during the pre-spring burning of field boundaries, slopes and other dry places.

Lasiocampa trifolii
Den. et Schiff.

Wsp ± 55 mm
Fpl Alfalfa, Clover, Trefoil, Blackthorn, Grasses

278

279

The eggs of the Lappet (279) measure nearly 2 mm. The female usually deposits them singly on leaves of trees. In captivity, the unfertilized eggs are laid gregariously. They have an interesting colour and pattern, and, furthermore, their surface also has a delicate, complex microstructure, visible only under a microscope. The illustration shows how the surface of some unfertilized eggs dries up and caves in. Fertilized eggs remain taut till the caterpillars hatch.

280

Lackey (280 — eggs, 281 — caterpillars, 282 — cocoon, 283 — moth) is a Euro-Siberian species *Malacosoma neustria* L. of wooded steppe, distributed in many forms up to the eastern parts of Asia, North Africa and North America. The changeable colouring **Wsp** ± 30 mm fluctuates between brown and reddish shades of ochre. The caterpillars **Fpl** Oak, Cherry, Plum, Birch, are gaily coloured. In the past it used to be a serious pest in certain Apple localities. The eggs hibernate.

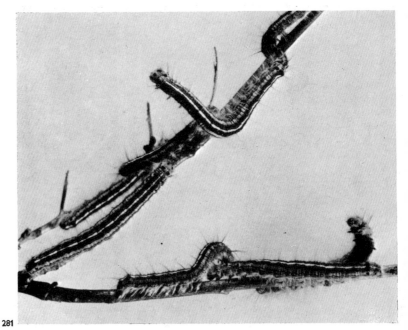

281

240

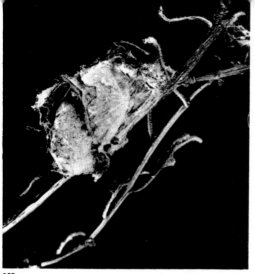

282

283

Drinker (284), a Euro-Siberian species, is yellow-brown and favours damp meadows and wood-*Philudoria potatoria* L. land clearings. The caterpillar hibernates. It is about 6 cm long, yellow with black spots and overgrown with black hairs. It needs plenty of water **Fpl** Grasses for successful development.

Wsp ± 55 mm

284

Chapter 11

THE ODD ONES OUT *Endromididae*
Brahmaeidae

After detailed study, butterflies and moths have been divided into families. These are mutually related groups of species, which share many common characteristics. Some families are indeed abundant — perhaps with thousands of species. But a few species do exist, which cannot be identified with any of the known families, and so a completely separate family was founded for them.

Kentish Glory (285 — male, 286 and 287 — female) is just such a moth inhabiting the Palaearctic *Endromis versicolora* L. region. The moths of the family Endromididae have a small head with large eyes, their antennae comb-like on both sides and their body covered in thick long hair. The proboscis is rudimentary. The venation of the wings shows a certain similarity to the Eggars (Lasiocampidae), and to the Attacidae and Bombycidae moths, also to the family Brahmaeidae. The attractive Kentish Glory is from a distance indistinguishable from a dead leaf. If resting on a tree trunk, it folds its wings in the shape of a roof over its body. The females, which are bigger and lighter-coloured

Wsp ± 55 mm
Fpl Birch, Hornbeam, Lime, Hazel

285

286

than the males, can be seen already in March in birch woods. The completely hairless, green caterpillar (288) with white stripes can be found in central Europe from May to June. Then it crawls to the moss and

pupates in a loose net cocoon. The pupa (289) hibernates and if the weather conditions are favourable, the moth emerges as early as February.

The moths from the family Brahmaeidae, which includes about 14 species, have, until recently, been seen only in Asia and Africa. A new species, discovered and described in Italy in 1963, extended the range of occurrence of this family also to Europe. In this book we have added this family to the chapter dealing with the family Endromididae, because they are alike in many characteristics and stand closely to each other in the evolutionary system. These are mostly larger moths with a very delicate,

wavy pattern on the wings, which makes all the species resemble each other. Another point of interest is the design of the outspread wing; under close examination, a substantial asymmetry of opposite sides of the wings comes to light in the distribution of tiny dots and lines. The body of these moths is powerful and large, the head comparatively small, the eyes big. The proboscis is rudimentary, but perhaps capable of sucking water. The caterpillars are hairless and gaily coloured, equipped in the earlier stages with long appendages.

Brahmaea wallichii Gray (290) occurs in the mountain forests of India. Picture 291 shows the underside of its wings.

Wsp ± 150 mm
Fpl *Phyllyrea*, Lilac, Ash, Privet

    Caterpillars of the family Brahmaeidae bear extraordinary chitinous outgrowths, the use of which has so far not been explained. Perhaps these twisted, spiral-like outgrowths have a frightening effect on an enemy when the caterpillar is moving. The outgrowths on the body of

291

the caterpillar of the *Brahmaea wallichii* species (293), are in comparison to the length of the body remarkably long and are attached in pairs to the second, third and the twelfth body segment. On the eleventh segment there is just a single outgrowth. When at rest, the caterpillar takes up a similar position to the Hawk-moth's caterpillar: it raises the forequarters of the body and keeps its head bent downwards. When

provoked, it flicks the free part of the body from side to side and is said to emit strange creaky sounds. The *Brahmaea* caterpillars live for some time in groups on various bushes and trees. They can be bred in Europe on lilac leaves. The larvae have the habit of holding to the twigs with their back side pointing downwards; to be shown more effectively,

Pupa's cremaster of
Brahmaea wallichii

our photograph pictures them with their heads up. In order to grow, the caterpillar must moult several times. It sheds the old skin which is not big enough and would cramp the growing body. A new, looser skin is by then already formed under the old one with the details of every organ, which has to function. It also must contain the rudiments of future coloration, which sometimes differs from the colour of the previous stage. For many hours or even days before this important event of moulting takes place in the caterpillar's life, it does not feed. Without moving, it stays firmly in one place, looking dead or ailing. The changes inside its body, the preparation of all the organs including all body openings and the development of the new network of cells — this all takes time.

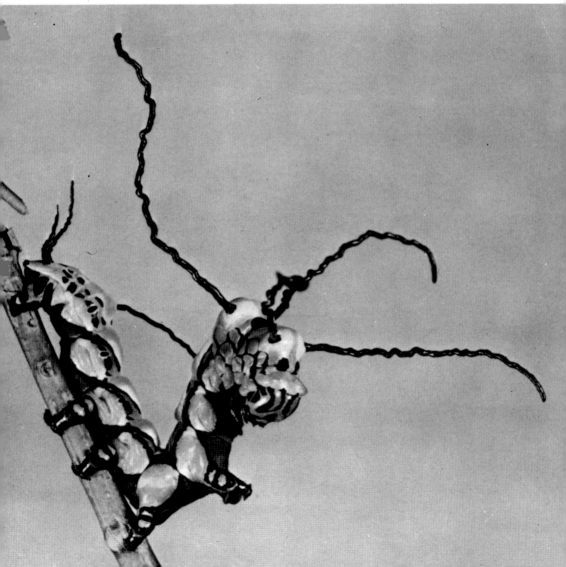

295

Then comes the moment when with the aid of flowing movements the old skin bursts somewhere round the head and almost imperceptibly starts to be pulled off the body. The various outgrowths and long hairs shed their skin too. The hard, glossy, peculiar horns of the caterpillar of *B. wallichii* also shed their skin and then they dry and ripen and take on a fresh colour (294, 295).

The fourth and final moulting of the caterpillar of *Brahmaea wallichii*

completely changes the appearance of the larva. All the 'ornamental' outgrowths are shed with the very last skin and we are confronted with
a completely different insect, but one which is equally interesting and
resembles a snake with the wide thorax behind the head. The brightness
of colours of a fully grown caterpillar probably puts most pursuers off,
so the twisted outgrowths become quite unnecessary (296, 297).

However, nature, which at times is so lavish, at other times so economi-
cal, makes sure nothing is wasted. As soon as the caterpillar revives from
the moulting and its biting organs harden, it devours the exuvia
without resting until all of it disappears (298). It obviously contains
valuable nutrients vital to the healthy development in the short life of
the future moth. The male lives about ten days, the female about 20 days
— or rather nights. When fully grown, the caterpillar of *B. wallichii* (299)
changes in colour from green to deep orange. It burrows into the soil
where it turns into a smooth, black pupa (292), from which, in captivity,
the moth emerges after a period of two months.

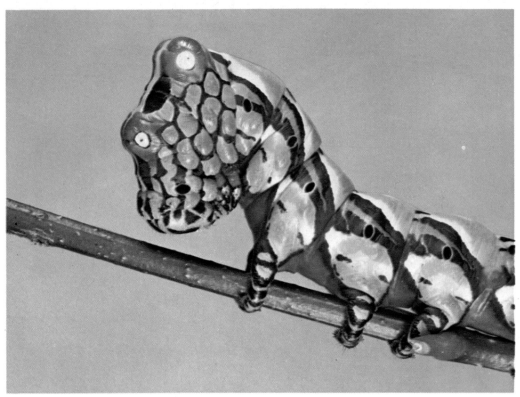

299

All moths of the family Brahmaeidae, distributed over Africa, Asia and Europe, closely resemble each other. Their most outstanding common feature is large areas on the margins of both pairs of wings, decorated with a series of parallel curves forming a fine wavy pattern. This design is particularly fine and dense in the moths of the African genus *Dactyloceras*.

Brahmaea hearseyi White (300 — male) is one of the Asian species. The illustrated specimen comes from the subtropical mountain forest in Assam (2,000 m above sea level). It resembles the preceding species differing from it only in some anatomical features and details in the design of wings. Young caterpillars have, in contrast to *B. wallichii*, hooked horns. This beautiful moth inhabits southern and western China, northern parts of the Indian subcontinent and some of the Sunda Islands. Its caterpillars undergo an unusually rapid development, pupate in the ground and the adult moths emerge in early mornings.

Wsp ± 135 mm
Fpl Syringa, Oleaceae

254

Acanthobrahmaea europaea Hartig (301, male) is a new species, described in 1963. This discovery was made in Italy, in the southern Neapolitan Apennines, on the
slopes of the once volcano Monte Volturino (height 1830 m).

Wsp ± 62 mm

301

The family of the Emperor Moths Attacidae (Saturniidae) embraces undoubtedly the most beautiful moths on Earth. They are distributed throughout all continents in about 1,200 species, most of which are tropical. Their wings are usually decorated with a 'peacock's eye' — a round, brightly coloured eyespot. These striking markings on the wings often have a frightening effect and help the defenceless moths to escape from insect-eating enemies. The Emperor Moths are of medium to large size, with a strong, hairy body, small head and rudimentary proboscis, which is useless for feeding. The caterpillars are hairless or more commonly equipped with tough hairs growing from wart-like tubercles. They pupate inside silk cocoons, which are either suspended, or lie on the ground.

Lesser Emperor Moth (303 — female, 304 — male) is a Euro-Siberian moth which is distributed
Saturnia pavonia L.   throughout wooded steppes of central and northern Europe and Asia as far as the Amur region. The male is smaller than the female, but is

Wsp ± 60 mm
Fpl Bilberry, Heather,
Hornbeam, Rose

more vividly coloured. The hind wings particularly are a bright rusty-yellow, whereas the basic colour of the female's two pairs of wings is dull and fairly uniform — a pinky grey. In contrast to other Emperor Moths, this species is active during the day. Picture 302 shows an adult caterpillar. The moths hibernate as pea-shaped pupae suspended from sloe or bilberry twigs.

302

Brood of the Lesser Emperor Moth

Firm cocoon with pupa of the Greater Emperor Moth

303

Greater Emperor Moth (305) is the largest European Emperor Moth, in fact the largest Lepido-
Saturnia pyri ptera species found in Europe. An inhabitant of wooded steppes of the
Den. et Schiff. Orient, it is found in the warmer regions of northern Africa, Europe and
Asia as far east as central Asia. The female pictured here came from
Wsp ± 125 mm the Bulgarian coast of the Black Sea; when fully extended, the wingspan
Fpl Blackthorn, Apple, Pear, can be as much as 157 mm.
Amygdalus, Vine, Walnut, Ash

257

Nail-mark (306 — male, 307, 310, 311 — females) is another moth with a partial daytime activity.

Aglia tau L.

Wsp male ± 50 mm,
female ± 85 mm
Fpl Beech, Oak, Lime, Birch,
Blackthorn, Alder, Willow,
Pear, Apple

During the warm spring days the male alone zig-zags through beech and mixed forests and his flight is very fast. The female flies by night, fluttering slowly and laying the fertilized eggs on young shoots. The female's light brown colouring and drab markings make her almost invisible when hanging during the day near the ground covered with dead leaves. The Nail-mark inhabits central Europe, the more southern parts of northern Europe and eastwards as far as Japan. In central

306

Europe it emerges from the hibernating pupa in April or May. The caterpillars (308) live from May to the beginning of August. They have an unusual shape: a white line divides the body into a yellow-green upper side and blue-green underside. Their outline is broken and resembles the dentated margins of leaves, among which the caterpillars hide. Before pupating, the caterpillars leave the green leaves and crawl to the ground, turning at the same time reddish-brown. They burrow into the leaves and moss, spinning a loose cocoon round themselves. The pupae are dark brown, with a dull wrinkled and rough surface, their end abruptly narrowing into a point.

Picture 309 shows a young caterpillar of the Nail-mark, which is covered with strange spiky outgrowths. Picture 310 illustrates the under-

308

side of the wings of this moth, which have the colour of dead leaves and bear a white mark in the form of the Greek letter 'tau'. The upper side (311) shows the triangular spot in the centre of the blue black-rimmed 'peacock's eyes'.

261

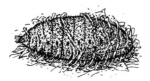

Pupa of the Nail-mark in a
loose cocoon

Robin Moth (312 — female) occurs in the temperate and warmer regions on the east coast of
Platysamia cecropia L.   North America. The brownish wings are traversed by a reddish-brown
band and their centres are decorated with whitish half-moon-shaped
Wsp ± 125 mm markings, which are pinkish at the edges. The front corner of each fore-
Fpl Sycamore, Willow, Rose, wing bears a dark bluish 'peacock's eye'. The green caterpillars often
Lilac, Apple, Plum, Blackberry, feed on leaves of fruit trees. This species is bred in many institutes
Oak, Alder, etc. throughout the world for experimental purposes.

Atlas Moth (313 — male) is one of the largest of all Lepidoptera. It is found in south India and
Attacus atlas L.   on the islands of southeast Asia, including Indonesia. This species has
many subspecies and forms. Plants of the families Simaroubaceae and
Wsp ± 235 mm Salicaceae are the favourite food of caterpillars.

Edwards' Atlas Moth (314, 315 — male) is slightly smaller than the preceding species but its
Attacus edwardsii
White

Wsp ± 190 mm
Fpl *Ailanthus glandulosa*

colouring is more distinct. Here the rusty yellow-brown colour of the wing is not dominant. The wings are inclined to be a deep chestnut brown, and the region around the central spots is almost black. The wavy yellow borders of the wing are very impressive and striking. The 'windows' — small areas without scales in the centre of the wings, are transparent, as in the preceding species, but the body is decorated in a white design. Even the underside of this attractive moth is lovely, with the borders of wings dusted in greyish-mauve, and altogether more colourful than the upper side (315). The damp, inaccessible valleys of the Himalayas are the habitat of this beautiful moth. Here their caterpillars feed on various deciduous trees.

314

315

Cocoon with pupa of the
Edwards' Atlas Moth

If we wish to breed these giant moths in captivity, it is necessary to obtain roomier cages and to accommodate each pupa separately. A beginner is always astounded when he sees such a giant emerge from the chrysalis, which itself does not appear over-large. Next comes the problem how to prepare such a giant for the collection without damaging it; an injection of ammonia is highly recommended. The third unpleasant reality is that even the spacious setting board is insufficiently large for such an enormous wing area. So it is important that everyone, who wishes to witness the unforgettable moments of the emergence of this giant moth and experience the excitement, must be well prepared. The pupa from which this species emerges, is relatively small. Shaped like a barrel and intertwined with leaves, it is often much smaller than the cocoon of the European Greater Emperor Moth. What emerges from

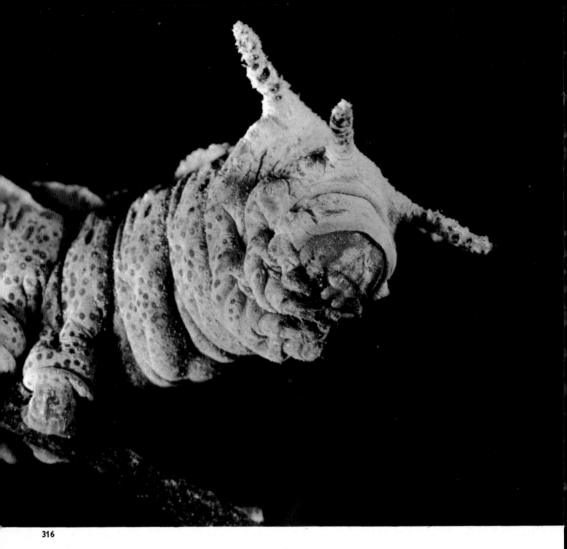

316

such a pupa, which is hardly larger than a hazel nut, is one of the wonders of nature. To ensure that a healthy, perfect moth develops, it is necessary to adhere to the following points: to moisten and water the pupa at the correct time and to ensure that the young moth will be able to climb the cage walls easily and hang from a sufficiently coarse surface of the ceiling. Glass walls of a cage are all too often the cause of permanent damage to the insect.

The adult caterpillar of this species (316, 329) is blue-green with deep blue dots at the sides of its body; large dots form two rows with smaller dots in between. The outgrowths behind its head have blue cross-stripes and dots. There is a large red spot on each outer area of the anal valve. The whole caterpillar, including the protuberance, is coated with whitish powder, similarly to some insects of the sub-order Coccoidea or Aphidoidea. The smaller caterpillars particularly are really smothered with the powder. Caterpillars of different *Attacus* species are fairly alike. Fully grown caterpillars measure about 10 cm and are almost immobile.

Graellsia isabellae Graëlls (317, male) is the only species of European Silk-moths whose hind wings extend into elongated spurs. It is transparent green-blue; the head, thorax and bands at the borders of the wings are a vivid yellow. The edges of the wings, and the distinct venation on the wings are pinkish red-brown on a live specimen. The eyespots in the centres of all four wings consist of yellow, blue, red-brown and black rings. A small, transparent window is in the middle. The range of this exquisite insect is restricted to an area in the mountains of Sierra de Guadarrama in central Spain, at the height of one thousand metres. It has also been seen in southern France, north of Marseille, in the valley of the river Durance.

Wsp ± 80 mm
pl *Pinus maritima* (all other Coniferae)

The light green caterpillars with tufts of hairs on their backs, a brown back stripe and lateral interrupted cross-stripes, live, in contrast to the other *Attacus* species, on conifers (pines). The conical pale-brown pupa measures about 29 mm and is enclosed in a translucent, thin, but fairly strong bag-shaped cocoon.

Moss cocoon with pupa of
Graellsia isabellae

317

318

Malagasy Silk-moth (318 — male) from the virgin forests of southern Madagascar, is one of the
Argema mittrei Guer. most bizarre, but most beautiful and valuable moths of the world.

Wsp ± 140 mm

Moon Moth (319, 323, 324) occurs in the more temperate regions of North America and to the
Tropaea luna L.   south as far as Central America.

Wsp ± 85 mm
Fpl Walnut, *Carya, Diospiros*

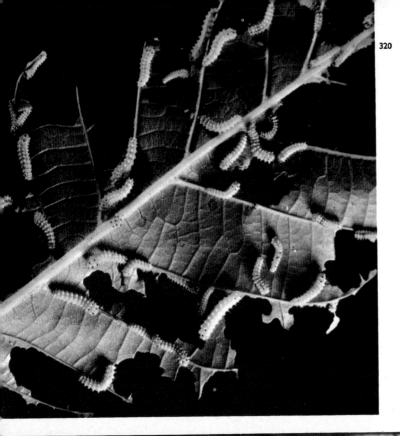

320

Cocoon with pupa of *Samia cynthia*

321

322

The Moon Moth's caterpillars (320, 323) are green with a red design. The moment they hatch from brown eggs they begin to feed on leaves of walnut trees. When bred in captivity, they are prone to virus diseases from which they do not recover.

Picture 319 shows freshly emerged Moon Moths spreading their wings in a quiescent position. They remind us of modern aeroplanes preparing for flight. The caterpillar (323) is beautifully coloured.

Samia cynthia Drury (321) is a Silk-moth of the Orient. It inhabits India and the Indo-Malayan
Wsp ± 120 mm
Fpl *Ailanthus*, Magnoliaceae,
Lime, *Cytisus*, Castor Oil Plant
region, where it occurs in various geographical forms. Some of these moths are olive-brown with yellow and violet-rose designs. The caterpillar (322) is powdered in white similarly to the *Attacus* species.

273

Isopa katinka Westw. (325) has its wings coloured in a magnificent yellow, decorated with brown, dark grey and pink stripes. The undersides of the hind wings have a small red stain in the front corners. This species is frequently seen in China. It is also known in northern India, where it is very abundant in July. The caterpillars are equally beautiful: brown with deep shading and black warts. The sides of the body have yellow spots.

Wsp ± 80 mm
Fpl *Cissus, Leea,* Vine

324

325

326

Actias isis South. (326 — male) flies together with a few other related forms in the Sunda islands and in the vicinity of the Greater Sundas. It is tinted reddish-brown with blotchy yellow spots. The caterpillars are big and green, covered with hairy outgrowths and tufts.

Wsp ± 130 mm
Fpl Mango, Walnut, *Carya*, etc.

276

327

Chinese Oak Silkworm (327 — female, 328, 332 — male) is distributed extensively through *Antherea pernyi* Guer.   Indonesia and Indochina and to the north as far as Japan and the Amur River. Today and especially in the past it has been the most widely used source of silk for the Japanese and Chinese production. Now and again this species has been successfully cultured in Europe and set free in nature. It is excellently camouflaged. The plump green caterpillar with the tufts of dark bristles and dark spots upon its reddish head has yellowish lateral stripes with a row of blue hairy warts underneath.

Wsp ± 105 mm
Fpl Oak, Beech, Sweet
Chestnut, Poplar, Willow,
Birch

Picture 329 shows the caterpillar of *Attacus edwardsii*, (see p. 266), coated in white powder.

277

328

Callosamia promethea Drury has a caterpillar with unique structures behind its head, which are quite exceptional in the insect kingdom. Its striking colouring proba-

Wsp ± 80 mm
Fpl Lauraceae (*Cerasus, Liriodendron*)

bly has a warning effect (330). The two sexes of the adult moths are distinctly different in coloration. The female is vividly coloured in hues of grey-brown, rust, black and white, whereas the male (see pen drawing on p. 280) is almost black with a pale grey border of the wings. This species inhabits North America, occurring in the states on the Atlantic coast from southern Canada to Florida.

Rothschildia orizaba Westw. (331) is one of the most beautiful moths of this genus. This truly

Wsp ± 110 mm
Fpl *Fraxinus americana* (Ash) (deciduous trees and bushes, *Cerasus*)

magnificent species flies in the hot regions of America, inhabiting Mexico and spreading to the north as far as Arizona. A number of its forms occur in the tropical areas of South America. The wings of these are decorated with large transparent windows, similarly to the *Attacus* species of the Old World.

329

330

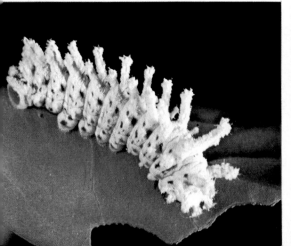

332

Picture 332 shows the front view of an enlarged head of the male Chinese Oak Silkworm (see p. 277) with its antennae.

Both male and female butterflies, those lepidopterans with simple clubbed antennae, are usually very active. We only need to recall the courtship flights of the Whites, or of any other butterflies dancing over the meadow! Both partners flutter round one another with equal grace and elegance and frolic in the air. Such species have a comparatively long lifespan; both males and females suck nectar from flowers providing them with energy for movement and reproduction. The eggs form in the female's branched ovaries; they gradually grow and ripen and when fertilized, are ready to be laid upon a foodplant.

Species which have only rudimentary mouth organs cannot accept food in their adult life. The adults cannot grow, and the insect must wisely and sparsely use the energy it accumulated during the caterpillar stage and brought with it when emerged. At that time the males' copulatory organs are literally packed with millions of microscopic sperms whose weight, however, seems no impediment in their wild flight. But the females, whose bag-shaped abdomen bears from birth the heavy load of tens and hundreds of eggs, are very limited in their capacity of movement. After emerging, they usually hang very near the place of emergence and wait for the male's arrival. He is lured by the product of the scent glands, which are placed most frequently at the end of the abdomen. The male can sense with his antennae the female at a distance of several kilometres and by night. There are about 40,000 nerve cells

Callosamia promethea – **male**

on the branched, bipectinated antennae, which come to a fine hair nerve point, jutting into space. If the male does not wish to tire through a long search, he can simply sit and wait for the wind to bring the desired scent of the female. He ignores other smells which are of no interest to the butterfly or a moth; the joint effort of the sensitive antennae and purposeful flight brings him to his destination.

Perisomena caecigena Kup. (333) is from southern Europe. The picture illustrates the antennae of the ochre-yellow male.

Wsp ± 70 mm
Fpl Oak

333

Indian Moth (334) lives in the southern parts of China and in Indo-Malayan countries including
Actias selene Leach Indonesia, where a number of similar and related species occur. The thorny caterpillar is at first brown with a wealth of spots, later green with yellow stripes and orange warts on the second and third body segments. The pale brown, thin and opaque cocoon is about 40 mm long; the pupa is brown, glossy with scarlet grooves, and is about 35 mm long. The emerged moths, particularly the males, are most susceptible to any disturbance. Then they press their legs against their body and beat their wings against the ground, till they are completely battered. It is advisable to feed the caterpillars in captivity with leaves of nut trees in the spring, and willow leaves before winter.

Wsp ± 110 mm
Fpl Mango, Walnut, Plum, Apple, *Carya*, Willow

334

335

In the temperate and hot parts of America there are nearly two hundred Emperor moths of the genus *Automeris*. These magnificent moths of medium to large size have their forewings without eyespots but decoratively shaded with a covering colour and a leaf structure. The males are smaller, lighter, but more vividly coloured. The hind wings are usually large, expressively and gaily coloured.

Bull's Eye Moth (335 — male) occurs in several forms in the United States and spreads to the *Automeris io* Fab. south up to Mexico. The vividly coloured caterpillars are well noted for inflicting damage on cotton and fruit plantations as they feed on apple, pear, plum, cherry and other trees. They have tufts of hairs (urticating hairs) which, when touched, sting like nettles.

Wsp female ± 90 mm, male ± 60 mm

283

Chapter 13 THE SILKWORM *Bombycidae*

The family Bombycidae consists of about 300 subtropical and tropical small-sized moths, most of which live in South and Central America. Only few species inhabit warm parts of Africa and Asia. Their forewings are sickle-shaped, the proboscis is absent, and the venation of the wings resembles that of the Emperor Moths. The caterpillar, which appears to be bald, has widened front segments and a small horn on the abdominal segments. It pupates in a firm, egg-shaped cocoon made of silk.

336

True Silkworm (336 — female, front view) is known for being monophagous. This moth has
Bombyx mori L. changed through 5,000 years of domestication so much, that it has lost
its ability to fly. Because of this the shape and the antennae of the two
Wsp ± 40 mm sexes do not differ much. The wild-living *Theophila mandarina* Moore
Fpl Mulberry is undoubtedly its original form.

The female lays a brood of about 500 eggs (337) often directly on
its own cocoon, or on nearby leaves. The freshly laid eggs are about
1.25 mm long, and their yellow colour turns greyish later. Caterpillars

339

(338, 339), which generally hatch after the winter, are at first dark, about 4 mm long and have a thick hairy coat. They resemble the larvae of the Emperor Moth. For thousands of years breeders have tried to vary the menu of the True Silkworm. But nothing but mulberries pleased the palate of these moths, who choose death rather than touch any other food. The heat-loving mulberry does not of course grow everywhere nor very quickly. The cultivation of *Bombyx mori* is therefore strictly dependent on the supply of mulberry leaves. The tradition of cultivating caterpillars for industry is thousands of years old and has today become a science, where all effort is directed to improve the quality and the length

of the silk thread and to safeguard the caterpillars from epidemics. The most serious of these diseases is 'pebrine' — the jaundice of the Bombyx moth, which is a deadly disease carried by moths and eggs of this species. It is caused by a parasitic protozoan. There is only one protection against this disease: strict cleanliness and a continuous microscopic control of egg specimens.

The cocoons of this Silkworm (340), from which the thread is unwound, are roughly 35 mm long. The length of the thread, whose diameter is about twenty thousandths of a millimetre, can be up to two kilometres but the pure thread suitable for making silk yarn measures about 900 metres.

The range of the five thousand species of the Tiger-moth family Arctiidae extends over all continents. They are small to medium-sized, bear similar designs on the venation of their wings and their antennae are not particularly long, usually thread-like, occasionally slightly combed. The caterpillars have sixteen legs, are covered with long hairs and very agile and quick. On the whole, these are rather lovely and harmless moths, some of them ranking among the most beautiful species.

American Weaver Tiger-moth
Hyphantria cunea
Drury

Wsp ± 30 mm
Fpl Mulberry, Sycamore, Elder, Apple, Pear, *Cerasus*, Blackthorn, Lime, Willow, Poplar, etc.

(341, a pair during mating) has wings sometimes plain white, sometimes darkly spotted. This small moth used to be a harmful pest of fruit trees in North America, and after the Second World War was also introduced in Europe. In countries with a temperate climate it can multiply alarmingly and cause a lot of damage, particularly to mulberry trees and nearly all fruit trees. The caterpillars of this Tiger-moth (342) at first live gregariously in a thickly woven nest on twigs, but later go

341

342

their own way. They pupate in cracks and crevices of fences and under the bark of trees in a loose, bag-shaped cocoon (343). The pupa hibernates.

A brood of the American Weaver Tiger-moth (344) can number as many as 500—1,000 eggs. The average measurement of each is 0.5 mm.

343

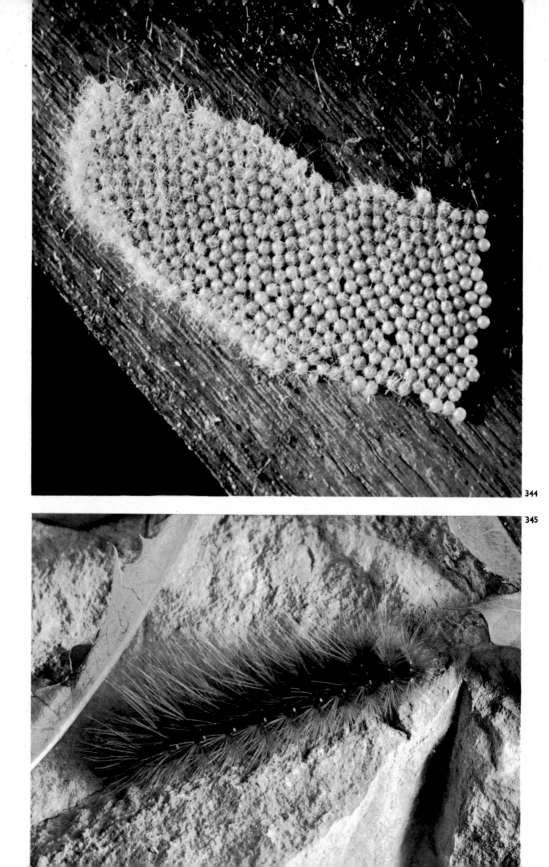

346

Garden Tiger (346) is a moth of the Holarctic wooded steppe common throughout Europe and the temperate areas of Asia as far as Japan. It penetrates high into the mountains and to the northern countries. It also occurs in North America. When the Garden Tiger is resting, its wings closed, the beautiful bright colours of the hind wings remain hidden. The fully grown caterpillar (345) hibernates and pupates in June of the following year. The moth flies at night during July and August.

Arctia caja L.

Wsp ± 60 mm
Fpl Dandelion, Clover, Blackberry, Vine, Walnut, Honeysuckle

291

347

348

349

Feathered Footman (347) as most European Arctiidae, demonstrates its vivid and contrasting
Coscinia striata L. colours. The yellow wings are decorated with black bands. This is
Wsp ± 35 mm a Euro-Siberian steppe species.
Fpl Hawkweed, *Salvia, Festuca*

Clouded Buff Moth (348) is yellow with red decorations. This is a Euro-Siberian species of the
Diacrisia sannio L. woods and steppes. Caterpillars feed on dandelion, bedstraw, nettle, etc.
Wsp ± 38 mm

Scarlet Tiger (349) is metallic green-blue with yellow and whitish markings. The hind wings
Panaxia dominula L. are purple with black spots. This is a species of the Orient found in
Wsp ± 50 mm deciduous forests and wooded steppe.
Fpl Nettle, Comfrey, *Lamium,*
Strawberry, Willow,

293

Epicallia villica L. (350, 351) inhabits central Europe where it keeps to the sunny slopes in the
Wsp ± 55 mm
Fpl Dandelion, *Lamium,*
Blackberry, *Lycium,* Achillea
wooded steppe. It is most numerous on the coasts of the Black Sea and in the east.

Brown Tiger-moth (352) is a Euro-Siberian steppe species, which seeks warm heather
Hyphoraia aulica L.
Wsp ± 35 mm
Fpl Hawkweed, Dandelion,
Euphorbia, Achillea, Vetch
growths and sunny slopes. The caterpillars of all the mentioned Tiger-moths hibernate.

294

351

352

The huge Noctuidae family of the Owlet Moths contains over twenty thousand species with a world-wide distribution, reaching even beyond the Polar Circles. In this most varied group, there are many species of small, medium, or large-sized moths which occur in the tropics. Also, the moth with the greatest wingspan of all the Lepidoptera in the world, the South American *Thysania agrippina*, belongs to this family. The majority of the Owlets are tiny, with inconspicuous grey and brown colouring. The forewings are triangular, the shorter hind wings can be folded. The antennae are thin, bristly and long, longer than half the length of the forewings. The proboscis it usually fully developed and functional; only exceptionally is it rudimentary. The larvae are generally bald, but some species are thickly haired. They are mostly night-feeders and pupate in the ground.

Buff Arches (353) is a Euro-Siberian steppe species. The forewings are decorated with a magnifi-
Habrosyne pyritoides   cent pattern of varied brown and grey hues, which have a silvery sheen
Hufn. (*H. derasa* L.)   while the moth is alive. This species represents the Tetheidae (Cymato-
phoridae) family, which, according to the most modern classification,
Wsp ± 38 mm   does not belong among moths.
Fpl *Rubus*
The subfamily Apatelinae is a member of the true moths — Noctuidae. These are very interesting moths with beautiful caterpillars.

353   354

355

Sycamore Moth (354, 358 — caterpillar) is grey and excellently camouflaged. This is a Euro-
Apatele aceris L. Siberian species of woods and wooded steppe. Caterpillars feed on horse
Wsp ± 45 mm chestnut, willow, poplar, hazel and sycamore.

Grey Dagger (355) is also well camouflaged, and distinguishable from the previous species by
Apatele psi L. the black dagger-like markings in the shape of the Greek letter 'epsilon'
Wsp ± 35 mm on its light grey forewings. The caterpillar (359) has a soft horn on its back.
Fpl Willow, Rose, Blackthorn

Knotgrass Moth (356, 360 — caterpillar) is a Euro-Siberian steppe species which has equally
Apatele rumicis L. flawless camouflage colouring as the two preceding species.
Wsp ± 35 mm
Fpl Dock, *Euphorbia*, Nettle

356

357 358

Alder Moth (357) is a
Apatele alni L.

Wsp ± 35 mm
Fpl Alder, Oak, Lime, *Cerasus*

very rare Euro-Siberian species of deciduous forests. The young caterpillar twisted to the shape of a question mark, imitates bird droppings.
As the larva grows (361), it takes on a warning black-blue coloration with
yellow stripes and glossy chitinous protuberances which among Palaearctic moths is unique. It pupates in rotted wood.

359

360

361

Scarce Merveille du Jour (362) has blue-green forewings with grey-brown design. This Euro-
Moma alpium Osbeck   Siberian species inhabits deciduous forests.

Wsp ± 37 mm
Fpl Oak, Beech, Elder

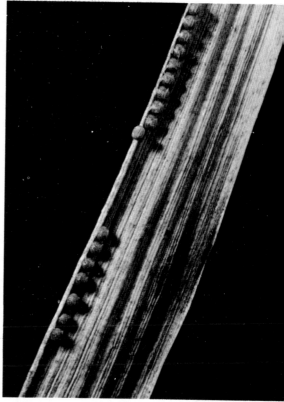

364

365

Large Yellow Underwing is a well-known, attractive Palaearctic moth. Picture 363 shows a part
Noctua pronuba L.   of its brood. There can be about 450 eggs, which hatch after seven to
eight days. Some hibernate and do not pupate till the following year.

Wsp ± 55 mm
Fpl Clover, Primrose, Violet,
Poaceae, Cabbage, etc.

Some moths, such as those of the *Plusia* and *Unca* genera, develop
bristles on their thorax and abdomen, consisting of long scales which
change to hairs and which help to break up the conspicuous outline of
a moth and imitate mud, for instance, lying on the grass by the path.
One such example is the following species.

Dark Spectacle Moth (364) is a Eurasian species of deciduous forests and wooded steppe. The
Unca triplasia L.   colouring of this moth is grey-brown, similar to mud or a dry, shrivelled
leaf.

Wsp ± 32 mm
Fpl Stinging Nettle

Green Sandgrass (366) is one of the most beautiful of European moths. This Euro-Siberian
Calotaenia celsia L.   steppe species is very rare and appears only exceptionally in dry pine
forests and sandy clearings. Each year, around the end of September, it
is possible to lure it to the light. Picture 365 shows the Green Sandgrass's
eggs laid under the rolled edge of the dry grass blade which makes them
inconspicuous. They were photographed after the blade was unwound
and dried out again. The eggs of this moth hibernate. The yellow-white,
almost bald caterpillar with black warts lives in hiding in grasses, where
it also pupates.

Wsp ± 42 mm
Fpl Bush Grass, Tufted Hair
Grass, Mat Grass, Sweet Vernal
Grass

366

Viper's Bugloss Moth
Anepia (Epia)
irregularis Hufn.

Wsp ± 30 mm

(367) is also rare in central Europe. Though distributed throughout all Europe as far as central Asia, it is strictly bound to calcareous or sandy slopes overgrown with the herbs it feeds upon (Spanish catchfly, larkspur, *Gypsophila*).

Agarista agricola Don.

Wsp ± 56 mm

(368) from eastern Australia is a typical example of the colouring of some of the exotic moth species. Caterpillars feed on vine.

Gold Spot Moth
Plusia festucae L.

Wsp ± 35 mm
Fpl Sedge, Reed Grass, *Alisma, Iris*

(370) has glossy, golden patches on the brown wings. It keeps to damp meadows and swampy ground, where its green caterpillar feeds on water plants; here the caterpillar also hibernates. This is a Eurasian species.

Some moths have exceptionally large dimensions, such as those of the *Nyctipao* and *Patula* genera from the Palaearctic regions of the Far East, which have huge 'peacock eyes' on their wings, or of the *Thysania* genus from South and Central America.

367

368

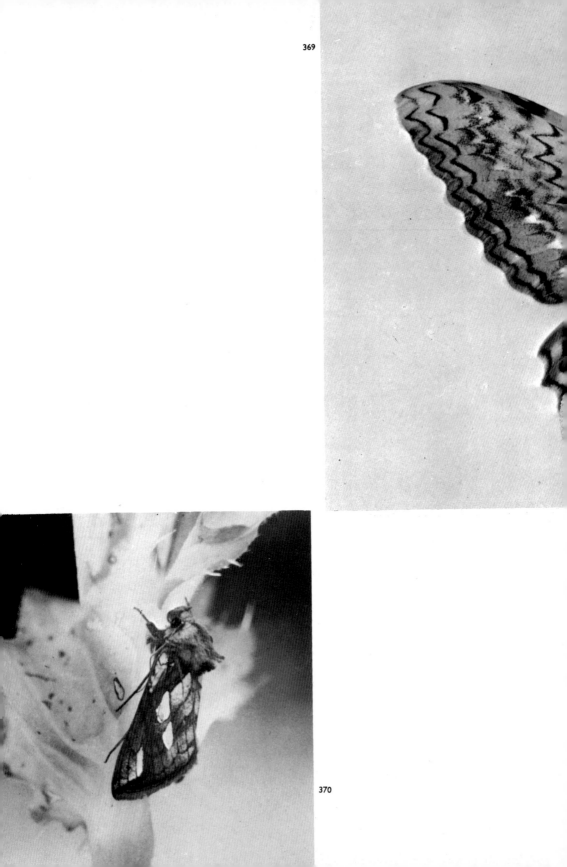

369

370

Thysania agrippina Cr. (369) with grey-brown coloration above and black and white spots
underneath, has the largest wingspan of all Lepidoptera in the world.
Wsp ± 270 mm Wingspans can measure 290 mm, and sometimes measurements of
300 mm are given. Such a gigantic moth is more like a bat or a night-
bird when seen under the cover of darkness.

Also in central Europe there is a rule which applies to moths: every
species has a defensive or warning coloration.

Scarce Wormwood Shark Moth (371) is a Euro-Siberian steppe species. Like its caterpillar
Cucullia artemisiae (372), it is hardly distinguishable from its foodplant (mugwort, *Matrica-*
Hufn. *ria*, tansy).

Wsp ± 39 mm

Grey Monk (374) is a rare oriental steppe species. Its caterpillar (373) has conspicuous warning
Cucullia campanulae Fr.   coloration.

Wsp ± 45 mm
Fpl Bluebell

373

Sandy or clayey cocoon with
pupa of a *Cucullia* sp.

374

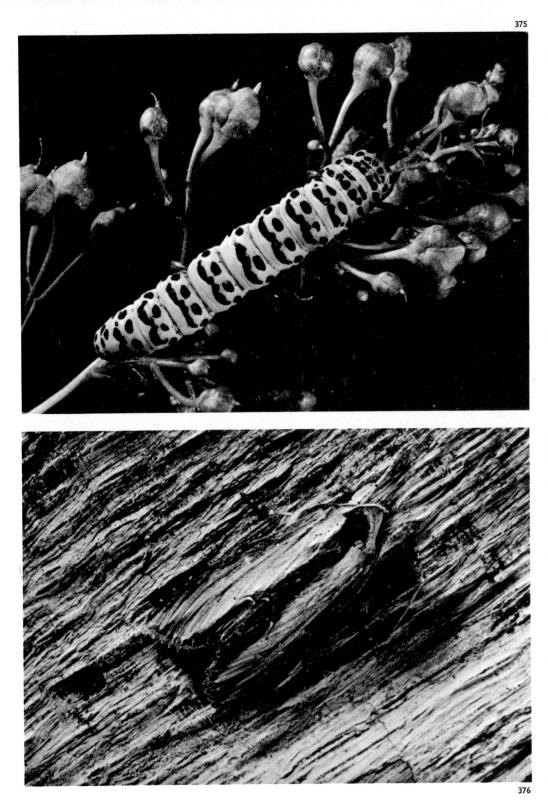

Water Betony Shark Moth (376) looks like a brown chip of rotted wood. It is distributed through-
Cucullia scrophulariae out all Europe to the east as far as Siberia. The caterpillars' warning
Schiff. colours (375) are very conspicuous on the high stems of figwort: they
have yellow spots and black lines on a greenish background.

Wsp ± 43 mm
Fpl *Scrophularia, Verbascum*

The Underwings are the most conspicuous moths of central Europe.
They are mostly large Noctuids with inconspicuously coloured forewings, but extremely vivid hind wings.

Clifden Nonpareil (377) is the largest Underwing, which has penetrated from central Europe
Catocala fraxini L. into the east as far as Japan. This is the only Palaearctic Underwing
with a blue stripe on the hind wings.

Wsp ± 90 mm
Fpl Oak, Ash, Willow, Picture 378 illustrates the eggs of the North American Underwing
Sycamore *Catocala neogama* Abb. et Sm., 0.95 mm in diameter.

309

**Pupa of the Clifden
Nonpareil**

Ephesia fulminea Scop. (379) has yellow cross-stripes on the hind wings. Most of the European
Underwings have red stripes.

Wsp ± 55 mm
Fpl Blackthorn, Plum, *Padus racemosa*, Oak

380

Burren Green Moth (380) is a Euro-Siberian steppe species, which inhabits wild bushy or *Calamia tridens* Hufn. grassy slopes. The wings are green, which is most exceptional and rare in moths.

Wsp ± 40 mm
Fpl Grasses

Herald (381) in adult stage hibernates in caves and cellars. It is an interesting Holarctic forest *Scoliopteryx libatrix* L. species.

Wsp ± 45 mm
Fpl Willow, Poplar

381

Chapter 16

THE WHITE PESTS *Lymantriidae*

Family Lymantriidae comprises of substantially more than two thousand species of moths, which, at first glance, look harmless enough. The majority is of medium size, but there is a number of smaller ones; only a few species can be called large. They resemble and are related to the Owlets, and sometimes remind us of the small Eggars. The male has broadly bipectinate antennae, the female's are more plain. Their proboscis is rudimentary, the head small. The colouring is sometimes completely white, or spotted and dull; species vividly coloured are only seen in the tropics. The caterpillars are very hairy.

Black Arches or **Nun** (382 — right — female, left — male), a Euro-Siberian moth, fond of woods, *Lymantria monacha* L. is one of the three Tussock-moths of the Palaearctic region which, from time to time, cause serious damage to the cultivated forest plantations in Europe.

Wsp ± 45 mm – male
Fpl Spruce, Pine, (Oak, Beech, Bilberry)

The white forewings bear a black-brown design, the hind wings are grey-brown, and the female's abdomen is reddish. The introduction of pine or spruce plantations in some of the central European countries caused the overpopulation of the Tussock-moth, particularly during the years

382

383

between 1917 and 1925. In July and August this overpopulation brought about catastrophic damage. The gradual introduction of the more natural mixed forest type arrested the disastrous occurrence of the Tussock-moth, but it is necessary to limit the numbers of this infester and keep it under observance.

384

385

White Satin Moth (385 — female) is silvery white. Occasionally it also undergoes a population
Leucoma salicis L.   explosion but only in poplar avenues or on individual trees. It is not
a feared pest in the localities where it occurs in Europe or in the cooler
Wsp ± 50 mm   parts of Asia. Its magnificent caterpillars (383, 384) live on poplars and
Fpl Poplar, Willow   willows, often communally, and pupate in spun leaves. The females lay
piles of eggs, which they cover with white stiffening foam. This protects
the eggs from the effects of winter. The caterpillars live in May and
June, and the moths emerge towards the end of June; they fly till July.
If the autumn is warm, the caterpillars hatch the same year and hibernate
while they are still small.

The Gipsy Moth (*Lymantria dispar* L.) is similarly coloured to the Nun,
but has less of the dark, zig-zag lines on the forewings, which makes
the moth lighter. The Gipsy Moth is also slightly bigger. The female
lays her eggs on bark in batches and covers them with a layer of rust-
coloured hair, which gives them the appearance of a fruiting body of
a bracket-fungus. The caterpillars have five pairs of blue warts on their
back, with red pairs behind them. This attractive moth is an old inhabitant of all Europe and Asia, and, in the east spreads to Japan;
occasionally it propagated en masse and damaged fruit trees. But its
natural enemies, such as the fifty species of Ichneumon flies, thirty
five species of the Garbage Ichneumons and Chalcidoids, over fifty

species of Caterpillar flies, Calosoma beetles, Carrion beetles, not to mention the cuckoo and virus diseases, these all have managed to keep the propagation of this species in the Old World in bounds. However, when introduced into the United States, it devastated over 250,000 hectares of forests.

The Brown-tail (*Euproctis chrysorrhoea* L.) is an oriental species of the wooded steppe. Originally it inhabited all central and southern Europe, North Africa, and in the east it reached Transcaucasia. In 1890 it was introduced to North America, where it caused extensive damage. In the Old World it has almost as many natural enemies as the preceding species.

Vapourer (387 — female, 388 — male) is a small, interesting moth. Its exquisite caterpillar (386) can be seen in spring and summer on leaves of wild plum, rose or sloe. The caterpillar measures less than 4 cm and pupates on a twig. It spins a loose cocoon and turns into a pale brown glossy pupa, which is endowed with exceptionally long hair on the back. The moths emerge about a month later. The male, its brown wings spotted in white, flies away from its cocoon during the first day. But the female hangs on the

Orgyia antiqua L.

Wsp ± 27 mm – male
Fpl Willow, Beech, Oak, Blackthorn, Plum, Rose, Spruce

387

388

389

empty cocoon, for her wings develop only into tiny stumps. This tiny 'sack' filled with eggs tempts the males for a distance of up to three miles by pushing out its scent glands in quick succession — about four times per second. After pairing, the female lays all her eggs — about 200 — usually over her own cocoon. The eggs remain on the twig over winter. They hatch usually towards the end of May, thus forming the first generation. The second generation flies in late summer.

Pale Tussock-moth (389 — male) is substantially bigger than the Vapourer. Its colouring is *Dasychira pudibunda* L. very variable, but consists usually of grey and brown shades. This Euro-Siberian moth inhabits Europe, northern Asia and western Siberia. Today **Wsp** ± 50 mm it is more frequently seen in deciduous forests, parks and gardens. **Fpl** Poplar, Willow, Horse During day it hangs on the bark. The females lay their eggs on the bark Chestnut, Walnut, Oak, Black- of trees in small, uncovered broods — about 250 eggs in the whole. The thorn, *Cerasus*, Apple, Rose, caterpillars (390) are among the most attractive in Europe. The shining Bramble yellow colour with the velvety black incisions and the purple hair-tufts

317

at the end of the body, plus the brushes of long hair on its back make it very conspicuous indeed. It lives from July to September. In September it spins a thin, loose cocoon, which is either greyish or yellowish, usually in the dry foliage on the ground. The pupa is glossy and translucent, in parts transparent, so the inner organs can be seen. It is honey-brown and the back side is covered with long hair. The caterpillar of the Pale Tussock-moth has very variable coloration, so it is possible to find it in colours of rust, red and even violet (391).

390

This is a very interesting family of nocturnal moths, which owe their name to the prominent scaly horn sticking out from the hind margin of each forewing, or possibly to the tooth-edged processes covering the back of many of their caterpillars. Such characteristics are not of course common to all the Notodontidae species, which number about 2,000. These tree-dwellers of small to medium size rest during the day with wings folded in a roof-like position. They are usually densely haired, particularly on the chest and abdomen. Their large head is often covered in hairy scales forming crests. This pattern is frequently repeated on the chest. The antennae of the male are shortly combed, of the female narrow, almost bristly. The proboscis is usually rudimentary. The forewings of the Prominents are mostly narrow, and so is their elongated abdomen. The coloration of the forewings is nearly always concealing, imitating shades of dead leaves, bark of trees, or wood chippings. Sometimes the forewings bear glossy patches in silver or gold. The caterpillars in some species and genera are bald, in others thickly hairy, and they have the most bizarre shapes of all Lepidoptera. In defence, they not only raise their head, but also the back third of their body; some shoot out a spray of burning liquid, others can bite effectively.

392

Chocolate-tip (393) is a Euro-Siberian species with dull grey-brown colours. Its caterpillar (392) *Clostera anastomosis* L. is very pretty. On its back it has a black band with white dots, on the sides it is decorated with yellow stripes and in front and in the back it has red protruding warts.

Wsp ± 35 mm
Fpl Poplar, Willow

Iron Prominent (394) had to be photographed against a green leaf, so it would be visible. When *Notodonta dromedarius* L. resting on tree trunks, its colour is so concealing, that it is difficult to see where the moth ends and the bark begins. It is seen in birch woods, but also inhabits thickets by woodland brooks near large meadows. In central Europe it flies in two generations, making its first appearance from May to June, the second from the end of July till the end of August. It is distributed from the eastern coast of the Atlantic across all Europe and western Asia to Transcaucasia and to the north into Siberia. This is one of the species whose forewings bear the tooth-like tufts of scales

Wsp ± 40 mm
Fpl Birch, Alder, Willow, Poplar, Hazel

projecting from the centre of the hind margin, which are visible when viewed from the side. The caterpillar of the Iron Prominent (395) is one of the most bizarre of all the Palaearctic caterpillars. If we are fortunate enough, we may find it on twigs of young birch or alder undergrowth, or on willows and poplar branches. It usually pupates in a cocoon on the ground or in the ground. The moth emerges the same year, or the pupa hibernates in the ground. It was given the Latin name of 'dromedarius' — camel, because of the humps on the caterpillar's back.

The most peculiar of all the European caterpillars – *Stauropus fagi*

395

396

Pebble Prominent (396) is a grey-brown Euro-Siberian nocturnal moth distributed in the
Notodonta ziczac L. Palaearctic region, whose ideal habitat is deciduous forest. As the caterpillars feed mostly on the undergrowth of willows, poplars and aspen,
Wsp ± 40 mm the adult moth is most frequently seen near rivers, woodland brooks and
Fpl Poplar, Willow humid forest gullies and pools. The attractive caterpillars are either
grey-red or grey-violet, and behind their small head which rests on
a thin neck are two tooth-like projections. They often raise the stumpier
back part of the body, thus forming the shape of the letter 'Z'.

397

Coxcomb Prominent (397) is a beautiful example of the protective colouring. It is yellow-brown, *Lophopteryx capucina* L. often even rusty-yellow. It is covered in a rich coat of scales on body and wings. The raised tufts of hairs form dentated margins of the wings.

Wsp ± 40 mm
Fpl Birch, Willow, Poplar, Sycamore, Oak, Lime

This moth can be seen in nature already at the end of April in open birch woods and in similar localities as the preceding species. It is also Euro-Siberian and reaches quite a way into the north and into the east across Siberia into Korea. Green colours predominate in caterpillars. They pupate in the ground.

398

399

400

Hybocampa terrifica Den. et Schiff. (= **Hoplitis milhauseri** F.) (399) is a rare Eurasian species, whose range extends to eastern Asia. Its caterpillar (398) is extremely bizarre with excellent protective colour and shape. It stays hidden in oak trees where it feeds from June till middle of August. Then it pupates in cracks of the trees it feeds upon, forming firm cocoons from the chewed wood splinters, so the cocoon in the bark completely merges with its surroudings. The cocoons are placed on old trees on the underside of strong branches. The pupae hibernate and the moths emerge at the beginning of May of the following year.

Wsp ± 45 mm
Fpl Oak, Birch, Beech

Poplar Kitten (400) is another Euro-Siberian Prominent which inhabits central Europe. It *Harpyia bifida* Brahm penetrates quite a way into the north, as far as southern Sweden, and into the east up to Mongolia. The caterpillars of this species (401) are somewhat different in shape than those of most other Prominents. The hind segments of their body end in a fork-like structure, which the caterpillars raise and open when provoked. These caterpillars are over 40 mm long and feed in July and August, mostly on aspen leaves.

Wsp ± 40 mm
Fpl Aspen, Poplar, Willow

Puss Moth (402, female above, male underneath) from central Europe is light grey with dark
Cerura vinula L.   grey design. The green caterpillar has a violet band behind its head and
                          on its back (404).

Wsp ± 60 mm
Fpl Willow, Poplar

Cerura erminea Esp. (403) is also from central Europe, but is slightly smaller and rarer. It is
                          a white moth with greyish design, distinguishable from the previous
Wsp ± 55 mm   species. The upper part of its abdomen is black. The caterpillar differs
Fpl Poplar, Willow (in tree   from the caterpillar of the previous Prominent by having the violet
crowns)   band tapering from the centre of the body towards the legs. Picture 404

329

404

Excited caterpillar of the Puss Moth

clearly illustrates the difference between the three pairs of thoracic legs under the head, from which the legs of the future moth develop, and the several pairs of abdominal feet, or prolegs, which, during pupation, lose their function and disappear. The caterpillars of both the last two Prominents are quite conspicuous in nature. Being 6 cm long, they are often seen on the stony or clayey banks of rivers amid willow bushes. When they are on guard and raise the forequarters of their body, the bold colours are very noticeable. Furthermore, these caterpillars are equipped with a similar organ to the one a spitting cobra uses for its defence. If provoked, a spray of burning liquid gushes out at its enemy from under the head, to a distance of 20 cm. The caterpillars have yet

405

another weapon, situated in the hind part of the body. They can suddenly raise their back and curl it over their head. Two red whips fly out of the fork-like tails at the end of the abdomen, which twist and turn around the head like snakes.

Buff-tip Moth (405) is yet another Euro-Siberian moth of deciduous forests with a wondrous *Phalera bucephala* L. coloration and shape. The light outline of the wings behind the head glistens with silver. The yellow-black caterpillars, striped longitudinally **Wsp** ± 55 mm with black head, feed in July and August; for quite some time they stay **Fpl** Oak, Birch, Lime, Willow, in a group, packed during the day side by side, most frequently on oak Poplar, *Alnus*, Elder leaves. They pupate in the ground, and the pupa hibernates.

Chapter 18   A WORD OR TWO ABOUT THE OTHERS

In the preceding seventeen chapters we have examined the most attractive representatives of the order Lepidoptera — the beautiful Swallowtails, the Whites and the Yellows, the Fritillaries, the Morphos and all the others. There still remains a number of other families, consisting of moths which at first glance are less attractive, more primitive in their development, and which we shall now briefly mention.

Early Thorn is a Eurasian species, with a caterpillar (406) typical of the moths of the large Looper *Selenia bilunaria* Esp.   or Spanner family Geometridae. This grey-brown creature, similar to
Wsp ± 40 mm
Fpl Lime, Willow, Elm   a dead twig, has six normal legs, but only four prolegs, and moves there-

406

Caterpillar of a *Geometridae*
species

fore with the 'looping', or 'spanning' movement characteristic of this
family.

Great Oak Beauty (407) is resting during the day on the bark of a tree, spreading its wings
Boarmia roboraria horizontally as is typical of Geometrids. This characteristic position, and
Schiff. their thread-like, bristly or combed antennae makes them distinguishable
from diurnal butterflies, which they sometimes resemble. This is a Euro-
Wsp ± 50 mm Siberian species; in the world there are more than twenty thousand
Fpl Oak, Birch, Beech, Elm Geometridae species.

333

Chrysiridia madagascariensis Less. (408, bottom left) is from Madagascar. The markedly
larger female is coloured vividly yellow and has a red-brown stripe across

Wsp ± 85 mm
Fpl Omphalea, Euphorbiaceae

its wings. Males are red-brown with a darker, oblique stripe. Each forewing bears two round whitish spots. The caterpillar cannot successfully
develop without drinking water. It pupates in a pale cocoon on the ground.

Urania leilus L. (408, top right) comes from Central and South America. These day-flying
butterflies occur in thousands. During their spring migration to the

Wsp ± 70 mm
Fpl Omphalea

north and late summer flight to the south they interrupt the quick,
zig-zag movement with sitting on wet rocks and plants to drink. Once
landed, they turn their head upside down and sit with outstretched
wings.

Alcidis metaurus Hpffr. (408, top left — female) is from north Australia. The *Alcidis* genus
Wsp ± 95 mm

is related to the *Urania* genus, its representatives inhabiting the tropics of Indo-Malayan region.

Alcidis aurora S.G. (408, bottom right — the male) is from New Guinea. All the mentioned species of the family Uraniidae are nocturnal moths with daytime activity — and are therefore day-flying moths. They fly with great expertise and elegance high in the crowns of trees, and resemble the Swallowtails. Their chubby, vividly coloured caterpillars with a coat of short hair pupate in a cocoon on the ground.

Wsp ± 75 mm

Zygaena angelicae Ochs. (409, top) has green, red-spotted forewings (wingspan ± 30mm) and red hind wings. Caterpillars feed on *Lotus* and *Coronilla*.

Zygaena carniolica Scop. (409, bottom) also belongs to the numerous family Zygaenidae, commonly called Burnets, which numbers roughly one thousand species, and is found in the warm and temperate zones of Europe, Asia, Africa and America. In America, the enormous family Syntomidae takes the

Wsp ± 25 mm
Fpl *Onobrychis, Dorycnium, Trefoil*

409

place of the Burnets, and comprises of tiny, primitive day-flying moths of a very similar type. Burnet moths used to be most abundant in central and southern Europe, but as they were dependent on original arid and steppe calcareous biotopes, many species died out or are dying out with the disappearance of such natural localities.

Oak Tortrix (410) can be easily seen against bark of trees. But their colour conceals them against
Tortrix viridana L. leaves. If, however, we brush against a branch of an oak during June, when they emerge en masse, hundreds of the disturbed, pretty green

Wsp ± 20 mm moths will fly off, settling down again almost immediately. Their fore-
Fpl Oak wings are smooth and green, the hind ones grey. The female lays eggs in pairs on twigs in the oak crowns. When, after hibernating, the cater-pillars hatch, they start to strip the oaks bare, attacking all new foliage

410

at the end of April or beginning of May. They pupate enveloped in a twisted leaf in an attached black pupa, from which the new moth soon emerges. Though this species has many enemies such as some birds and insectivorous insects, occasionally a population explosion results in a gradual weakening of trees, which are then very prone to infections of parasitic fungi.

Apple Tortrix (411) is today cosmopolitan and has a completely different existence to that of the *Cydia pomonella* L. preceding species. We are acquainted with this species from the frequently worm-eaten apples. These two members of the Tortrixs are only negligible examples of the vast family Tortricidae, which consists of about 4,500 species, some of which are serious infesters.

Wsp ± 15 mm
Fpl Apple, Pear, *Cydonia*,

411

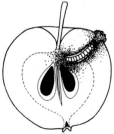

Caterpillar of the Apple Tortrix

Goat Moth (413)
Cossus cossus L.

Wsp ± 80 mm
Fpl Willow, Poplar, Birch,
Elder, *Padus*, *Cerasus*, Apple,
Pear, Blackthorn, Alder, Elm,
Mulberry, Vine

inhabits the warmer and the temperate part of the Palaearctic region and is one of the new European representatives of the Cossidae family, which numbers about 450 species. Its caterpillar (412) looks like a large fat worm, as big as a finger, which might have come out of a worm-ridden apple or plum. Even its colour is similar, for it is red like fresh meat and has a strong, sour smell of oak or beech wood. This caterpillar, which measures up to eight centimetres, does not, however, attack fruit, but wood. It lives first in groups under the bark of living trees; after the first hibernation, it lives alone, boring a passage into the wood. It hibernates twice or more times before pupating in a cocoon made of splinters and sawdust. If, during the felling of trees in winter, we find caterpillars,

412

413

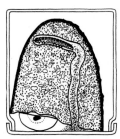

Emergency breeding of caterpillar of the Goat Moth

we can breed an adult Goat Moth from them. They will be only too pleased to bore their way into a large chunk of bread (it must be dark, rye bread), which must be placed in a covered glass bowl, to help the necessary dampness. We can make sure of this by placing a piece of fruit under the bread. The bread should be changed a week or two weeks later. It does not matter if it goes mouldy. This species is comparatively rare, for it has many enemies, such as the nightjars, owls, bats, Ichneumon flies and some parasitic fungi. Apart from this, when young, the caterpillars eat one another.

Many-plume Moth (414) is one of the strangest examples of all Lepidoptera. With about another
Orneodes
grammodactyla Z.
hundred species it belongs to the family of the Many-plume Moths, Orneodidae. These moths are mostly small and drably coloured, but each one of their wings is divided into six or more fine, feather-like structures, so it can be said, that instead of wings they have twenty-four 'feathers'. If we study more closely how the original wings have been split, we will see that the splitting is often incomplete. Individual 'feathers' are variably joined together at the root, but on the whole the appearance is the same and we are faced with a small moth which has feathers instead of wings. This Many-plume Moth is an oriental steppe species, largely dependent on some of the original plants of the steppe country. From southern and central Europe its range extends to the east into Asia Minor and Transcaucasia. The moth flies in two generations in May to June, and then towards the autumn. Some genera are said to hibernate in adult stage. The caterpillars live in the underground or ground tumours of sprouting plants; when they leave the root at the beginning of May, they spin a cocoon and pupate on the ground.

Wsp ± 15 mm
Fpl *Scabiosa ochroleuca* (and some other plants of the *Scabiosa* genus)

Plum Moth (415) represents the numerous family Alucitidae (= Pterophoridae). It is far bigger
Alucita pentadactyla L.
and much more conspicuous than the tiny grey Many-plume Moths. There are at least 600 species of this small moth distributed throughout

Wsp ± 25 mm
Fpl *Convolvulus, Calystegia,* Rose, Blackthorn, *Rhamnus*

414

the world. If in June or July we take a stroll through tall grass, or if we brush against a branch of a low bush, we may notice a slight movement, as if a tiny snow-flake had fallen from somewhere into the grass. But it easily grasps the blade with its long legs and stays put, its wings spread out. Then slowly it moves both the legs from the sides to the body. These two families are fairly distant from each other within the system of small moths, but their imagos are very alike at first glance. The Plum Moth is noticeable because it is snow-white all over. It is a Eurasian steppe species, which is distributed from central Europe to Asia Minor, Armenia and southwest Siberia. The greenish caterpillar, which measures about 15 mm, has tufts of short hairs on its warts, and feeds from August till May on different plants. It hibernates in hiding.

Hornet Moth (416) is
Sesia apiformis Clerck

Wsp ± 40 mm
Fpl Poplar, Willow

the biggest European species of the family Sesiidae or Clearwings, which comprises of about 800 species. These primitive moths mimic various stinging and inedible insects. The Hornet Moth mimics a Hornet. This is a Euro-Siberian moth, whose larvae are almost bald and burrow into the wood of poplars on which they feed. The moth emerges in May, and the caterpillars live from the summer, through two winters into the spring of the following year — so they take about three years to be full grown. Hornet Moths are heliophilous.

341

416

Adela degeerella L. (417) is a moth with a golden glitter and amazingly long antennae, which can be seen in open humid groves from May to July sitting on flowers. This is an oriental heliophilous species of deciduous forests.

Wsp ± 20 mm
Fpl Anemone

Primitive Moth (418), a golden-winged European moth, hardly a couple of millimetres long, *Micropteryx calthella* L. belongs to the Micropterygidae family, which consists of about eighty species of the most primitive moths. The mouth parts of this family are not modified to form a long coiled proboscis. Instead there are functional

Wsp ± 8 mm
Fpl Mosses and Liverworts

417

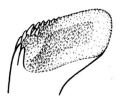

Mandible of the Primitive Moth with chewing surface

418

mandibles and the maxillae, which form the proboscis in all other Lepidopteran families, are short and adapted for holding pollen on which these moths feed.

Orange Swift (419) is a member of the family Hepialidae or Swift Moths. About three hundred
Hepialus sylvina L.   species of the Swifts live in countries with temperate and mainly tropical
Wsp ± 33 mm   climate. The inhabitants of the temperate zones are generally small
Fpl Plantain, Dock, Lettuce

419

420

moths, whereas some of the tropical species have a wingspan of up to 240 mm and many excel in wondrous beauty of design and coloration. Nearly all have an elongated, cigar-shaped body, with wings usually narrow but rounded, which have a simple and primitive venation; their antennae are short. The caterpillar of this species can be a harmful garden pest to vegetables and flowers. It is glossy grey-white with a pair of black warts on each segment. There are only single red bristles protruding from the warts, otherwise the caterpillar is almost bald. It is very agile and moves equally swiftly forward and backward. It pupates in the ground in a tubular cocoon, which resembles the cocoon of the Caddis Fly larvae. The moth flies at night from June to September. The caterpillar hibernates and pupation occurs in the spring.

Ghost Moth (420) is another representative of the Hepialidae family and its largest European
Hepialus humuli L. member. This is a Euro-Siberian steppe moth, whose range extends in the east into Asia Minor. Sometimes it is stated to be a pest of hop
Wsp ± 60 mm
Fpl Dandelion, Dock, Grasses, plants. This is because the caterpillars of all Swift Moths feed on the
Hop, *Daucus, Canabis* roots of plants, mostly of weeds however . . . The male is glossy white with a pink edge to its wings and the female is yellow with red oblique stripes on her wings. This moth lives in damp meadows, particularly in the foothills. The caterpillar hibernates.

344

BIBLIOGRAPHY

Barrett, C.; Burns, A. N.: Butterflies of Australia and New Guinea. N. H. Seward, Ltd., Melbourne, 1951

Bergman, A.: Die Großschmetterlinge Mitteldeutschlands I−VII. Urania Verlag, Jena, 1952−55

Bingham, G. T.: The Fauna of British India including Ceylon and Burma. London, 1905−07

Bourgogne, J.: Ordres des Lépidoptères; Grassé: Traité de Zoologie, vol. 10, Paris, 1950

Common, I. R. B.; Waterhouse, D. F.: Butterflies of Australia. 1972

Corbet, A. S.; Pendlebury, H. M.: The Butterflies of the Malay Peninsula. Oliver and Boyd, London, 1956

D'Abrera, B. F. R. E. S.: Butterflies of the Australian Region. Melbourne, 1971

Danesch, O.; Dierl, W.: Schmetterlinge. Belser Verlag, Stuttgart, 1965

Döring, E.: Zur Morphologie der Schmetterlingseier. Akademischer Verlag, Berlin, 1955

Ehrlich, P. R.; Ehrlich, A. H.: How to Know the Butterflies. Wm. C. Brown Co., Iowa, 1961

Esaki, T.: Coloured Illustrations of the Butterflies of Japan. Osaka, 1955

Ford, E. B.: Butterflies. Collins, London, 1946

Ford, E. B.: Moths. Collins, London, 1955

Forster, W.: Beitrage zur Kenntnis der Insectenfauna Boliviens. Zool. Staatssammlung, München, 1955

Forster, W.: Biologie der Schmetterlinge. Franckh'sche Verlagshandlung, Stuttgart, 1954

Forster, W.; Wohlfahrt, T. A.: Die Schmetterlinge Mitteleuropas. Franckh'sche Verlagshandlung, Stuttgart, 1955−60

Gerasimov, A. M.: Gusenicy (Caterpillars); Fauna SSSR. Moscow, 1952

Goodden, R. C.: Les papillons. Librairie Larousse, Paris, 1972

Harz, K.; Wittstadt, H.: Wanderfalter. Die Neue Brehm-Bücherei, Heft 191. A. Ziemsen Verlag, Lutherstadt-Wittenberg, 1957

Hemming, F.: The Generic Names of the Butterflies; Bulletin of the British Museum, suppl. 9, London, 1967

Higgins, L. G.; Riley, N. D.: A Field Guide to the Butterflies of Britain and Europe. Collins, London, 1970

Hodges, R. W.: The Moths of America North of Mexico. E. W. Classey Ltd., 1971

Howe, W. H.: The Butterflies of North America. Doubleday Comp. Inc., New York, 1975

Hrubý, K.: Prodromus lepidopterorum Slovaciae. Vyd. Slovenskej akadémie vied, Bratislava, 1964

Klots, A. B.: A Field Guide to the Butterflies of North America. Houghton Mifflin Co., Boston, 1951

Koch, M.: Wir bestimmen Schmetterlinge I−IV. Neumann Verlag, Radebeul und Berlin, 1961−63

Kurentsov, A. J.: The Butterflies of the Far East USSR. Nauka, Leningrad, 1970

Lee Chuan-Lung: Hudie. Peking, 1958

Lewis, H. L.: Butterflies of the World. G. G. Harrap and Co., London, 1973

Michener, C. D.: The Saturnidae of the Western Hemisphere; Bulletin of the American Museum of Natural History, vol. 98, 1952

Mitchell, R. T.; Zim, H. S.: Butterflies and Moths. Golden Press, New York, 1964

Munroe, E.: The Classification of the Papilionidae; The Canadian Entomologist, suppl. 17. Ottawa, 1960

Portier, P.: Biologie des Lépidoptères. P. Lechevalier, Paris, 1949

Ruffo, S.: Farfalle. Aldo Martillo, Milano, 1960

Schwarz, R.: Motýli (Butterflies) I−III. Academia, Prague, 1949−53.

Seitz, A.: Die Großschmetterlinge der Erde I−XVII. A. Kernen, Stuttgart, 1907−32

Shirozu, T.; Hara, A.: Early Stages of Japanese Butterflies in Colour. Osaka, 1960

Spuler, A.: Die Schmetterlinge Europas I−IV. E. Nägele, Stuttgart, 1908

Swanepoel, D. A.: Butterflies of South Africa. Maskew Miller Ltd., Cape Town, 1953

Tabuchi, Y.: The Alpine Butterflies of Japan. Hobundo, Tokyo, 1959

Urguhart, F. A.: The Monarch Butterfly. University Press, Toronto, 1960

Van Son, G.: The Butterflies of Southern Africa. Pretoria, 1949—55

Verity, F.: Le farfalle d'Italia I—V. Marzocco, Florence, 1940—53

Williams, C. B.: The Migration of Butterflies. Oliver and Boyd, London, 1930

Williams, J. G.: A Field Guide to the Butterflies of Africa. Collins, London, 1969—73

Wiltshire, E. P.: The Lepidoptera of Iraq. Adlerd and Son, Ltd., London, 1957

Wynter-Blyth, A. M.: Butterflies of the Indian Region. The Bombay Natural History Society, 1957

INDEX

Roman figures refer to text pages, figures in italics indicate numbers of illustrations.